DEATH'S
RED TAPE

DEATH'S RED TAPE

Your Guide for Navigating Legal, Financial, and Personal Transitions When a Partner Dies

MARK COLGAN

Certified Financial Planner Board of Standards, Inc. (CFP Board) owns the certification marks CFP, CERTIFIED FINANCIAL PLANNER, and CFP® in the United States, which it authorizes use of by individuals who successfully complete the CFP Board's initial and ongoing certification requirements.

COPYRIGHT © 2022 MARK COLGAN

All rights reserved.

DEATH'S RED TAPE
Your Guide for Navigating Legal, Financial, and Personal Transitions When a Partner Dies

ISBN	978-1-5445-2924-0	*Hardcover*
	978-1-5445-2923-3	*Paperback*
	978-1-5445-2925-7	*Ebook*

CONTENTS

Preface ix

1. Take Care of Immediate Concerns 1

2. Collect Survivor Benefits 27

3. Get Organized and Sort Through the Paperwork 49

4. Review Assets 59

5. Pay the Bills 67

6. Process and Manage the Estate 75

7. Understand Your IRA Distribution Options 93

8. Attend to Personal Affairs 97

9. Avoid Identity Theft 111

10. Estate Planning Essentials 129

11. The Soft Side of Your Estate Plan 135

12. Prearrange Your Funeral 153

13. Say Yes to Life 163

    Afterword 169

    Acknowledgments 171

    Additional Resources 173

    Glossary 177

    Index 185

    About the Author 189

*I dedicate this book to my beloved late wife, Joanne.
During our lifetime, we had a lot of good times
that created wonderful memories, never to be forgotten.
She was a courageous and giving soul with a smile
that could stop time. My continuous reflection
on our life together and her distinctive ways will forever
influence me to be a better man.*

PREFACE

A WEEK BEFORE 9/11, MY WIFE JOANNE DIED. HER SUDDEN DEATH intensified my awareness that life can be taken away at any moment. In the midst of my shock and grief, I had to contend with several unwelcome logistics. It started with funeral arrangements and death notifications. It continued with administrative tasks and revisiting my financial affairs. Even a CERTIFIED FINANCIAL PLANNER™ professional like myself had a hard time concentrating.

My tumultuous experience is unfortunately not uncommon. Through this book, I will help you navigate the logistics that follow a partner's death. This way, your loss won't be compounded by missed opportunities, costly mistakes, and missteps.

WHAT THIS BOOK IS ABOUT

Whether you're a surviving spouse, partner, child, another family member, or friend, *Death's Red Tape* provides you with valuable information to guide you through the financial and administrative process following a loved one's death. In particular, this book addresses the financial and legal issues that occur within the first six to twelve months after their death. To help you focus on the important issues at the appropriate time, I've organized and titled the chapters of this book to depict this timeline.

The following pages, and especially the checklists, give you a quick and easy way to educate and organize yourself during this period of transition. I've also added a glossary to help you understand the technical conversations you may have with attorneys, accountants, and government agencies.

Throughout the book, I also reference websites that will prove valuable to you as you obtain specific information about insurance, benefits, and preventing identity theft. These sites are listed in the Additional Resources section at the back of the book.

THE PURPOSE OF THIS BOOK

This is no time to procrastinate. Despite the grief and numbness you might feel right now, you are a survivor. Read on to start taking charge of your life. Once the nitty-gritty details of your loved one's death are under control, you can begin to heal and rebuild.

The loss you've experienced is unique and incomparable to any other. While it seems like there's no handbook, process, friend, or family member that could begin to understand what you're going through, opening your heart to the people and organizations around you may help you take steps toward grieving fully and making a better future for yourself. Keep an open mind while letting your precious memories sustain you through this difficult period.

MY OWN SURVIVOR EXPERIENCE

My wife, Joanne, and I had an incredible relationship. Besides having the best friendship anyone could ask for, we shared the magic of a loving marriage. My life was blessed.

Even so, Joanne and I experienced the challenges life so often brings. One of these challenges, as a result of Joanne's congenital heart disease, was that our lifestyle had to be a bit more relaxed than many. The simple things in life—activities like going for a walk or shopping at the mall—often had to take a back seat to her fatigue and need for rest. Still, these minor sacrifices were insignificant in comparison to the good times we shared. Joanne had a wonderful laugh and a way of making sure we made the most of everything. Anyone who knew her was familiar with her contagious laugh.

Joanne's challenges escalated as her heart complications progressed, however. In 2000, after six years of marriage, her condition worsened. When she developed pneumonia, we found ourselves speaking with doctors about heart transplants.

Even though they didn't feel she needed one at the time, we started the application process. The waiting list was two to five years, and they thought Joanne might need a new heart within that timeframe. Interestingly, while her condition was critical, they felt there was no immediate threat to her life.

The year 2001 was a roller coaster. While the New Year was marked with optimism for recovery and better health, it ended tragically. Toward the end of that summer, when it seemed Joanne had begun feeling better, she died.

On the morning of Tuesday, September 4, after a spontaneous and fun-filled weekend with her family at the lake, Joanne unexpectedly passed away. Even though we had no idea her death was imminent, our last moments together were very peaceful. I can vividly remember seeing her sitting lakeside in a lawn chair, gently leaning back with her eyes closed, basking in the afternoon sunshine. All the while, she was surrounded by her loving family. The experience taught me to never forget the fragility of life and how important it is to spend your time wisely. Do more of what you love and share it with those closest to you.

The hours following Joanne's death were dramatic. Within minutes of her passing, I found myself amid a crowd of people. I was surrounded by emergency medical technicians, firemen, policemen, relatives, neighbors, and the medical examiner. Within hours of her death, I was writing her obituary, selecting her casket, and planning the details surrounding her funeral. Then, later that day, I was purchasing a gravesite for both of us and even designing her headstone. Between the time the sun rose and set that day, I had gone from waking up with my wife to beginning the process of burying her.

Preface

My life was changed forever. It went from a wonderful life to one of tremendous, unbearable pain. I walked a path of introspection and carried on an internal debate about my purpose in life.

During this most difficult time, I also had to deal with the mountain of financial details that sprung up. Some might think that for a CERTIFIED FINANCIAL PLANNER™ professional like myself, such details would be easy to deal with. But, like you, the press of my emotions left little room for logical and practical thinking.

I remember asking myself, "If this is difficult for me, a professional in this business, how does someone who isn't a financial expert feel?" It was in this discovery process that I decided to channel my energy into helping others by writing this book and making a commitment to helping my clients at Montage Wealth Management.

MY MESSAGE TO YOU

My heart goes out to you in this confusing chapter of your life, but I want my message to you to be one of hope, not sorrow. My journey after Joanne died was not easy, and at times I felt I'd never be happy again. Fortunately, my emotions of fear proved to be misleading.

Today, I live an amazing life. Married to another wonderful woman, together we have two children. To top it off, we have three loving animals, two black Labs and a cat. My daughter says I'm too YOLO (You Only Live Once) for my age, but hey, we get one shot at this experience on earth. I am humbled to say that I am living proof that you can find happiness despite monumental loss.

May you also channel the energy of your loved one's life into your own so you become empowered and enjoy a future of promise and fulfillment.

1

TAKE CARE OF IMMEDIATE CONCERNS

Even while the news of this death is still fresh in your mind, you'll be called upon to contact funeral homes, financial advisors, insurance agents, attorneys, and family members. You'll also have to start making important decisions.

Perhaps you're one of the lucky few whose loved one detailed not only important information about their financial and benefits history, but also how they wanted to celebrate their life, including funeral arrangements, interment, memorial services, and charitable contributions. If not, you may not know where to start.

In addition to facing a mountain of paperwork, new terminology, and important decisions that may affect generations of your family, you may be struggling with grief. Your grief can include overwhelming emotions, which can make it difficult to concentrate on money, property, and other details that aren't the first things on your mind and in your heart.

If this is how you feel, you're not alone. Grieving people often have a hard time concentrating. No matter how smart or intellectual you may be, the emotions of grief may dominate and make focusing on mundane tasks close to impossible.

I originally wrote *Death's Red Tape* because, even though I was a CERTIFIED FINANCIAL PLANNER™ professional, the emotional toll of losing Joanne impaired my ability to handle all the financial, legal, and administrative tasks that sprung up in the aftermath of her death.

People grieving the loss of a loved one, whether they're survivors, parents or children, are prone to making substantial errors in judgment because their brains aren't firing on all cylinders. With this in mind, I strongly suggest that in any of your meetings with bankers, financial advisors, attorneys, and other advisors, you bring along a trusted friend or relative—one you have empowered to listen, take notes, and ask questions on your behalf.

IMMEDIATELY FOLLOWING DEATH

Notify the Authorities

If death occurs somewhere other than a hospital or nursing home, call 911 immediately. The police and medical professionals will determine the next step.

Notify Important People and Institutions

After relatives and friends have been notified, you or someone close to you should contact the following people:

- Organ bank/hospital (see details below)

- Funeral director and, if applicable, clergy

- Deceased's employer and business associates

- Professional advisors such as their attorney, financial advisor, insurance agent, and accountant

- Executor/executrix of the will or estate

If Applicable, Arrange to Donate Deceased's Organs

Typically, within the first twenty-four hours of death, one or more organs can be donated. Doctors decide at the time of death if someone is a good fit for this.

If the situation warrants, determine if the deceased wished to be an organ donor. First, see if they are officially registered. Check your state registry via the Health Resources & Services Administration at www.organdonor.gov. If they are not registered, don't give up. They may have taken a less formal approach and recorded their wishes on their driver's license, on an organ donor card, or maybe even on their mobile phone. Apple, for instance, has a "Health" app that allows people to register with Donate Life America.

You should also know that there is no cost to donate organs. Insurance companies or the people who receive the organ donation pay those costs. Also, organ and tissue donation is supported by most major religions in the United States and is considered a final act of love and generosity toward others. Throughout the entire process, the deceased's body is treated with care, respect, and dignity. And open casket funerals are usually possible for organ, eye, and tissue donors.

IN THE DAYS FOLLOWING

Go Ahead and Use the Decedent's Car

In some states, the immediate family of the deceased may continue to use their car until the deceased's registration and/or insurance expires. Contact your local department of motor vehicles to verify this.

Keep Track of Visitors, Gifts, Donations, Flowers, and Cards Received

The days immediately following your loved one's death are often filled with a flurry of activity and a parade of well-wishers. It may be difficult to respond at the time you receive notes, cards, donations, and gifts. So, ask a friend or family member to help you keep track. Knowing who sent what will help you later when you do have the time and desire to respond to these acts of kindness.

In addition to your own list, don't forget to keep a guest book at the wake and funeral so you retain a record of who came to pay their respects. You may find yourself referring to this information for many years to come.

Prepare for the Memorial Service/Funeral

Check for any prearrangements for funeral and/or burial

While a funeral director will take care of most funeral and burial arrangements, you'll want to check for any possible prearranged written funeral or burial instructions your loved one had recorded.

These wishes may be kept with the will in a safety-deposit box or they might be on file with an attorney or local funeral home. If your loved one was technically savvy, they may have recorded these details with internet-based services such as everplans.com or mywisdomwill.com. In some cases, the funeral arrangements may also have been prepaid.

Be prepared to pay for funeral expenses

Most funeral homes and cemeteries require their expenses to be paid prior to the service. Some will accept a life insurance assignment, but they may charge an added fee for doing so.

Take advantage of veterans and other benefits

Veterans, military service members, and their dependents can be buried in a national cemetery for free or possibly receive an allowance toward funeral and burial expenses. Other benefits may include obtaining a free ceremonial American flag, a headstone, and/or presidential memorial certificate. For more details, inquire with the National Cemetery Administration.

Other funeral benefits may be available through insurance policies, employers, the Federal Employee's Retirement System (FERS), or the Civil Service Retirement System (CSRS).

Check airline bereavement fares

Be aware that airline bereavement fares vary from airline to airline but have been eliminated in most cases (or are more expensive than going online to purchase tickets).

Protect your house against burglary

Funeral services and visitations are often publicly announced online and in local newspapers, increasing your risk of break-in and burglary. Thieves may search these listings and social networking sites, such as Facebook, Twitter, and Instagram. It's best to have someone remain in the home, if possible.

If there are items of significant value in the home, consider notifying your local police department of your absence, particularly if the funeral is taking place in another city. You might also consider putting your valuables in a safe-deposit box or storing them at a friend's house.

Get the tax deductions you deserve

According to the IRS, most individuals won't qualify to claim a deduction for funeral expenses unless they were paid for out of the funds of the deceased's estate. Keep in mind that many estates don't actually use this deduction, since most estates are less than the amount that is taxable.

Decide on burial or cremation

If you choose burial:

Check to see if your loved one already owns a burial plot—If they purchased a burial plot in advance, they'll have had a burial plot deed issued to them. Contact the funeral director or designated cemetery to determine whether a copy of the burial plot deed will be required to bury the decedent. Deeds may often be stored in a safe-deposit box at your bank or other secure location.

Contact the designated or desired cemetery—If a plot hasn't yet been acquired, consider buying two side-by-side plots now for you and your loved one. You may also want to buy plots for each member of your family. Too often, people wait to do this and by the time they get back to the cemetery, the adjoining plots have been sold. Also, you might get better pricing if you buy the property in advance of your need for it or buy multiple plots at once. It also must be said that what makes sense today may not tomorrow. The dynamics of life evolve, and even those close to you may prefer a burial elsewhere or no burial at all. Balance these perspectives to make an informed decision.

If you choose cremation:

Cremation is chosen much more often than it used to be and is likely to continue to be a viable option. Here are some considerations:

How to arrange for cremation—Cremation arrangements can be made through a funeral director. You'll be asked to select an urn (a container for the ashes) at the same time.

Cremation still allows for traditional services—If you choose cremation, don't overlook the fact that traditional services—including viewing and visitation with the casket present—are still possible.

Decide what to do with the ashes—You may choose to have the ashes placed in an urn kept in a private location, stored in an aboveground niche at the cemetery, or even buried in a cemetery plot. In some cases, more than one urn could be buried in a single cemetery plot, so you might start thinking about what you'd like to do for yourself. Alternatively, some people choose to bury ashes at a gravesite. Scattering of ashes is popular but viewed as illegal by most towns.

Whatever you choose, keep in mind that the ashes can be separated to fulfill more than one desire. Before making any irreversible decisions, discuss the options with close family and friends. If no conclusive decision arises, consider tabling such important decisions until later.

Obtain Death Certificates

Have the funeral director provide you with as many death certificates as you're likely to need. They can help you determine how many must be certified vs. copied.

The death certificate is used as proof of death for administering the estate, collecting life insurance, changing bank accounts, transferring titles and deeds, obtaining discounted bereavement airfare for relatives flying into town for the funeral, etc. Make sure to carefully check the information for accuracy and store the certificates in a secure location. Also, be aware that some states charge as much as $150 for one death certificate.

You can also obtain death certificates from the state's department of Health Services, Public Health, Vital Records, Health Statistics, or similar office (depending on your state).

Notify Social Security Administration

Funeral directors often report deaths to the Social Security Administration (SSA) as part of their services. Although paper forms are still available for notifying, the funeral director may prefer the Electronic Death Registration, a web-based system that aims to deliver death information to the Social Security Administration with greater speed and accuracy.

Ultimately, it is the survivor's responsibility to ensure that Social Security is notified of a beneficiary's death as soon as possible. So be sure to check with the funeral director, or you can call Social Security at 800-772-1213. You can also contact your local Social Security office.

IN THE NEXT WEEKS

Notify Credit Bureaus

If you are the spouse of the deceased person or a representative legally authorized to act on the person's behalf, you can ask to have a deceased notice placed on their credit report by calling the agency or by mailing in a copy of the death certificate along with the following information about the deceased:

- Legal name

- Social Security number

- Date of birth

- Date of death

Take Care of Immediate Concerns

Also include your name, your mailing address to send final confirmation, and a copy of your identification, such as a driver's license or other government-issued identification.

If you are not the spouse of the deceased, you will also need to include court documents authorizing you to legally act on their behalf.

Mail the required information to:

> Equifax Information Services LLC (800-685-1111)
> P.O. Box 105139
> Atlanta, GA 30348-5139
>
> TransUnion (800-888-4213)
> P.O. Box 2000
> Chester, PA 19016
>
> Experian (888-397-3742)
> P.O. Box 9701
> Allen, TX 75013

Meet with an Attorney

You may already have an attorney to work with to process the will and estate. If not, this is the time to find legal representation. Choosing the right attorney is critical. Many attorneys, especially the good ones, don't do a lot of marketing; they attract clients by word of mouth. To find these attorneys, you'll have to tap into their network of clients and colleagues. You might, therefore, consider the following search methods:

- **Ask other professionals**—Ask the attorneys and accountants you work with to recommend an estate attorney they know and trust.

- **Ask clients**—Satisfied clients can be a good source of referrals, but exercise caution. Clients aren't always the best judge of a professional's quality of work, especially in complex legal matters. You don't want a bad attorney with a charming personality.

- **Search legal directories**—You can search lawyers.com, which has an online version of the Martindale-Hubbell directory by legal specialty and geographic location. If you don't have internet access, check at your local library.

- **Contact your local bar association**—Go to www.findlegalhelp.org and click on your state to find a list of referral sources, such as your state or county bar association. Focus on referral sources that meet ABA standards. This means that they operate solely in the public interest and don't charge for referrals.

Consider the attorney's fees

Some attorneys may charge by the hour or a flat fee; others charge a percentage of the value of the estate. In some cases, a paralegal may do much of the paperwork and will have a different billing rate. You should inquire about the division of labor and the related costs.

Check for area of specialization

Martindale-Hubbell, the company that publishes a directory of attorneys in the United States, identifies four specialties related to financial planning:

- **Trusts and estates**—This includes estate planning and preparation of wills, trusts, and other planning documents.

- **Wills and probate**—Most attorneys do one or both of these. Transactional attorneys handle the administrative side of probate, while probate litigators represent clients in estate claims.

- **Eldercare**—This rapidly growing area of law specializes in the needs of older people.

- **Family law**—These attorneys handle divorces and all matters relating to children, including adoption, guardianship, child custody, and child support. They also do prenuptial agreements.

Meet with an Accountant

It's important that, as the surviving spouse, partner, or other family, you spend some time with an accountant. There may be tax returns due, estimated taxes to pay, or other items that need to be taken care of as the estate is awaiting settlement.

You may even want to consider a joint meeting with the attorney and accountant. It can be well worth the expense in creating clarity, organizing the things that need to be done, and getting things rolling.

Contact the Executor/Executrix

This person, named in the will, is the one responsible for executing the wishes of the decedent and processing the estate, including the distribution of assets to individuals and charities. The executor will work closely with the attorney and should be contacted immediately.

The executor/executrix of the estate may be you, the surviving spouse/loved one, an adult child, or another friend or family member.

Contact the People Listed as Witnesses in the Will

Many wills executed in the last thirty years are "self-proving." This means you don't have to locate the witnesses to prove the will is valid. If you aren't sure if your loved one's will is self-proving, ask your attorney.

If the will isn't self-proving, or if you anticipate a contest of the will, you'll need to locate the individuals who served as witnesses and whose names and signatures appear at the end of the document.

Take Care of Immediate Concerns

If Applicable, File the Will and Petition

If the deceased's estate is small or if the assets were owned in joint name, then you may not even need to file a will and go through the probate process.

Some states allow an estate to bypass probate if the estate is under a set amount; the assets in such a case are transferred with the use of a small estates affidavit. Although the procedure may vary from state to state, this method of transferring the assets of the deceased will save the heirs time and money over having to file a full-blown probate proceeding.

If everything was jointly owned or automatically passed to you or others by automatic beneficiary designation, there is no need to administer the estate through probate court. Even if the deceased and his spouse owned their home with rights of survivorship in their deed, then his entire share of the real property transfers to his spouse at his death with no action required in probate court. If the joint owner wants to later sell or mortgage the property, then most often all that will be required will be proof of death of the deceased joint owner.

Let's say that neither of these scenarios applies and you determine that a will must be filed. This must be done in the probate court in the county where the deceased died.

The petition is a formal request to be assigned as the executor and the will proves this. Probate proves that the will is genuine and then distributes the property and other assets according to the terms of the will.

Even if you don't have to probate the will, some states require the person who has custody of the will to file the will with the court to preserve it. This doesn't require opening a probate administration. But it will ensure that if after-discovered property, which would have been subject to probate, is found years after the decedent's death, they will be available to administer that property.

Acquire the Contents of the Deceased's Safety-Deposit Box

If you had a safety-deposit box in joint name with your loved one, you may open and empty the contents of the safety-deposit box. If the box was in the decedent's name alone, you'll need a death certificate and certificate of appointment from surrogate's court to gain access.

Once at the bank, an officer will accompany you into the vault, point out the location of the box, and insert one of the two keys needed to open the box. You'll need to bring the other key, which was given to the box owner.

You should decide whether to continue the box rental or terminate it at this time.

Take Care of Immediate Concerns

IN THE MONTHS FOLLOWING

Consider Postponing Major Financial Decisions

Recovering from a loved one's death is a dual process. In addition to the emotional toll, you also face financial issues that may have a big impact on your lifestyle. While taking control of your finances is an important step in rebuilding your life, don't rush into anything.

Most financial advisors recommend you not make any major changes or long-term decisions about finances for at least six months to one year after your loved one's death. Perhaps the most common of these major financial decisions is whether or not to sell your home. Such permanent decisions like this one are better made after a period of time has gone by, when you'll be able to think more logically rather than emotionally.

Maintain Cash Reserves

Cash flow should be your foremost concern at this time since it will have a direct impact on your lifestyle. Set aside sufficient cash for at least one year of ongoing living expenses, especially those new or one-time expenses that will likely need to be satisfied during this extended decision-making period, including attorney's fees and possible estate taxes. There may also be some surprises along the way, so save a bit more than you think you'll need, just in case.

Make a Detailed Budget

Make a detailed list of your income sources and expenses. For the first year or so, revisit it every three months to adjust either the budget or your living style appropriately.

The following sample worksheet is one you might consider using:

EXPENSE	AMOUNT
HOUSING	**AMOUNT**
Mortgage, rent and/or line of credit	
Property and school taxes	
House or renter's insurance	
Internet and phone (not cable TV or cell phones)	
Water, gas & electric	
Maintenance (HOA fees, repairs, lawn, etc.)	
Housing total:	
TRANSPORTATION	**AMOUNT**
Loan or lease payments	
Insurance	

Take Care of Immediate Concerns

Gas	
Maintenance/Other	
Transportation total:	

FOOD	AMOUNT
Groceries	
Pet food	
Dining out and lunch at work	
Food total:	

PERSONAL EXPENSES	AMOUNT
Recreation (club/gym memberships, hobbies, etc.)	
Entertainment (Netflix, cable, movies, theatre, sporting events, etc.)	
Personal (clothing, health and beauty)	
Childcare/babysitting	
Education: tuition, loans, rent, etc. (not 529 savings)	
Cellular phones and tablets	
Travel	

Payments against old credit card balances (not current/routine expenses)	
Personal expenses total:	

HEALTHCARE	AMOUNT
Medical insurance (not paid pre-tax from your paycheck)	
Copays, prescriptions, etc.	
Pet healthcare	
Healthcare total:	

INSURANCE TO PROTECT LIFESTYLE	AMOUNT
Life insurance	
Disability and long term care insurance	
Insurance total:	

GIFTS AND CHARITABLE CONTRIBUTIONS	AMOUNT
Gifts (including birthdays and holidays)	
Charitable contributions	
Gifts and contributions total:	

"PHANTOM" OR OTHER MISCELLANEOUS EXPENSES	AMOUNT
Random stuff difficult to account for	
Other expenses	
Other expenses total:	
TOTAL EXPENSES	

Check for Unclaimed Funds

It's not unusual for people to lose track of various bank accounts, tax refunds, stock dividends, etc. The result is billions of dollars sitting in unclaimed property funds, waiting to be taken by its rightful owners. To see if the deceased, or yourself for that matter, has any unclaimed funds, go to unclaimed.org. The site is run by the National Association of Unclaimed Property Administrators. You can either search on Missing Money, a multistate search engine, or connect to your state's individual site, where you can search for unclaimed money. Perhaps you'll find a pleasant surprise.

MAKE TIME TO GRIEVE AND CELEBRATE

While all the above concerns should be addressed, it's also imperative you make time to grieve and celebrate the life you had with your loved one. Whether it's through viewing old pictures, writing in a journal, surrounding yourself with family, or writing a poem—listen to your heart and embrace the rituals you deem appropriate.

Below is a poem I wrote the night Joanne died. It was my way of communicating my gratitude and love. Perhaps you, too, may find comfort in this poem or in one you write yourself.

MY DEAR JOANNE

I pray to you tonight with love,
our hearts still as one.
While your touch may not be near,
the company of your soul I hold dear.

Until we meet again,
let the heavens surround you with light
and all of the beautiful treasures
to which you claim right.

And as I finish my journey on Earth,
may God give me strength
and you give me hope,
for a new tomorrow I must cope.

Take Care of Immediate Concerns

**You are the sun in my day
and the moon in my night.
You are the inspiration
that brings me life.
I love you forever.**

—Mark Colgan

DEATH'S RED TAPE

TO-DO LIST

- ❏ Notify the authorities.
- ❏ Notify important people and professionals.
- ❏ Consider organ donation.
- ❏ Keep track of visitors, gifts, and cards received.
- ❏ Check for any prearrangements for funeral and/or burial.
- ❏ Check for veteran's or other burial benefits.
- ❏ Decide on cremation or burial.
- ❏ Protect your house against burglary.
- ❏ Obtain death certificates.
- ❏ Arrange to meet with an attorney.
- ❏ Arrange to meet with an accountant.
- ❏ Contact the executor/executrix of the estate.
- ❏ Contact the witnesses listed in the will.
- ❏ Find the will and petition the probate court.

Take Care of Immediate Concerns

❑ Acquire the contents of the safe-deposit box.

❑ Consider postponing major financial decisions.

❑ Maintain adequate cash reserves.

❑ Make a detailed monthly budget.

❑ Check for unclaimed funds.

2

COLLECT SURVIVOR BENEFITS

THIS CHAPTER WILL HELP YOU DETERMINE WHETHER YOU'RE entitled to certain survivor benefits and, if so, what you can expect and how to apply for them.

SOCIAL SECURITY SURVIVOR BENEFITS

Social Security benefits are paid to surviving spouses, their minor or disabled children, and sometimes other family members. Contact your nearest Social Security office as soon as possible to find out if you qualify. While the funeral director usually notifies the Social Security Administration, that isn't a formal claim for benefits.

Determining Decedent's Insured Status

If you're inquiring about whether you can collect survivor benefits, it's important to first determine if the decedent was currently insured or fully insured. This "insured status" is a determination of whether there's a benefit to collect.

For the decedent to have achieved *currently insured* status, they must have had at least six quarters of earnings covered by Social Security withholding during the full thirteen-quarter period prior to their death.

For the decedent to have achieved *fully insured* status, they must have had up to forty quarters (ten years) of earnings covered by Social Security, depending on their age at the time of their death. Additionally, if the decedent worked for only one and a half years in the three years just prior to their death, benefits can be paid to their children and spouse, who is caring for the children.

The decedent's insured status doesn't affect the amount of the benefit their survivors receive. It's simply a minimum work requirement, which must be met before a particular benefit is payable. Once this minimum is met, a benefit amount is computed based on the decedent's average earnings.

Who Can Collect Survivor Benefits

Certain relatives of the decedent have the opportunity to collect Social Security survivor benefits, potentially including the survivor, divorced survivor, unmarried children, and/or dependent parents.

Survivors

A survivor who did not remarry before turning age sixty (fifty if disabled) are eligible to receive survivor benefits:

- At full retirement age (full benefits)

- As early as age sixty (reduced benefits)

- At age fifty or older if disabled

- At any age, if she or he takes care of a child of the deceased who is younger than age sixteen or disabled

Divorced Survivors

A divorced ex-spouse who is at least sixty (fifty if disabled) can also collect survivor benefits if he or she was married to the deceased for at least ten years. Remarrying after turning sixty (fifty if disabled) has no effect on survivor benefits. But if you wed before reaching that age, you lose eligibility for survivor benefits on the prior marriage.

Unmarried children

Unmarried children can receive benefits if they are:

- Younger than age eighteen (or up to age nineteen if they are attending elementary or secondary school full time)

- Any age and were disabled before age twenty-two and remain disabled

Under certain circumstances, benefits also can be paid to stepchildren, grandchildren, stepgrandchildren, or adopted children.

Dependent parents

Parents sixty-two or older who received at least one-half support from the deceased can receive benefits.

Types of Social Security Survivor Benefits

In this section, we address survivor benefits, which are based on the earnings record of the decedent. This shouldn't be confused with spousal benefits, an entirely different set of benefits based on the earnings record of a living spouse. As for survivor benefits, there are two types.

One-time death payment

If the decedent was currently or fully insured, a $255 lump sum is payable to the survivor or dependent child generally eighteen or younger who was living with the decedent at the time of death.

Whether or not there was joint residency, this lump sum may still be collected if the survivor or children are immediately eligible for monthly benefits. If there is no eligible surviving spouse, the deceased's child (or children) may be eligible to receive the $255 lump sum. You must apply for this payment within two years of the date of death.

Monthly survivor benefit

If the decedent was currently or fully insured and you qualify, you may begin collecting monthly income survivor benefits.

People often ask, "Can I collect my deceased spouse's Social Security and my own at the same time?" The answer is that you may be able to get some of both but not the total of both combined. You receive the higher of the two. This means if the deceased's benefit was greater than yours, you will now receive your Social Security benefit plus an extra amount needed to equal the survivor benefit. For example, if your monthly Social Security benefit is $2,500 and your spouse's was $3,000, then you will be eligible for your $2,500 plus another $500 survivor benefit for a total of $3,000.

In select situations, maximum family benefits might also apply. There's a limit to the combined benefits survivors and their family members can receive each month. The family maximum is generally 150 percent to 180 percent of the deceased worker's benefit. Typically, the family maximum comes up when the decedent was the primary income earner, leaving behind a surviving spouse who is raising children who are also entitled to survivor benefits. It could also be an issue if the survivor is already collecting a government retirement or disability pension.

As you can see, there are several possible scenarios, each with its own associated rules, so it's highly advised that you get more details from www.ssa.gov and consult with a representative of the Social Security Administration.

How to Apply for Survivor Benefits

If you're not currently receiving benefits from the Social Security Administration, you should apply for survivor's benefits promptly as, in some cases, they aren't retroactive. Even if you're already getting retirement or disability benefits, unless they're on your deceased loved one's record, you may still need to apply for survivor's benefits.

When you're ready to begin the process—online, by phone, or in person—make sure you are prepared. Don't delay filing your claim just because you don't have the required data and documents. Be ready to answer the following questions and have as many of the required documents as possible:

- Your name and Social Security number

- Your name at birth (if different)

- The deceased's name, gender, date of birth, and Social Security number

- Your date of birth and place of birth (US state or foreign country)

- Your deceased child's date and place of death

- Whether a public or religious record was made of your birth before age five

- Your citizenship status

- Whether you have used any other Social Security number

- The state or foreign country of the worker's permanent residence at the time of death

- Whether you or anyone else has ever filed for Social Security benefits, Medicare, or Supplemental Security Income on your behalf (if so, they will also ask for information on whose Social Security record you applied)

- Whether the deceased ever filed for Social Security benefits, Medicare, or Supplemental Security Income (if so, they will also ask for information on whose Social Security record they applied)

- Whether you became unable to work because of illness or injury at any time within the past fourteen months (if so, they will also ask you the date you became unable to work)

- Whether the deceased was unable to work because of illness or injury at any time during the fourteen months before their death (if so, they will also ask you the date they were unable to work)

- Whether you or the deceased was in active military service before 1968 and, if so, the dates of service and whether you have received or are eligible to receive a pension from a military or federal civilian agency

- Whether you or the deceased worked for the railroad industry

- Whether you or the deceased ever earned Social Security credits under another country's Social Security system

- Whether you qualify for or expect to receive a pension or annuity based on your own employment with the federal government of the United States or one of its states or local subdivisions

- The names, dates of birth (or age), and Social Security numbers (if known) of any of your or the deceased's former spouses

- The dates of each of your marriages and, for marriages that have ended, how and when they ended

- The dates of each of the deceased's marriages and how and when they ended

- The amount of the deceased's earnings in the year of his or her death and the preceding year

- Whether the deceased had earnings in all years since 1978

- Your earnings for this year, last year, and estimated earnings for next year

- Whether the deceased had a parent who was dependent on the deceased for half of their support at the time of their death or at the time the deceased became disabled

- Whether you were living with the deceased at the time of their death

- Whether you have any unsatisfied felony warrants for your arrest or unsatisfied federal or state warrants for your arrest for any violations of the conditions of your parole or probation

- The month you want your benefits to begin

For more information, call the Social Security Administration at 800-772-1213 (TTY: 800-325-0778). This number provides you with automated telephone services to get recorded information and conduct some business twenty-four hours a day. You can also speak to a local Social Security representative. You can find your nearest Social Security office at www.ssa.gov/locator.

OTHER GOVERNMENT BENEFITS

If the deceased was employed by the government and you are a potential beneficiary, be sure to check into whether or not you may qualify for Federal Employee's Retirement System (FERS) benefits, Civil Service Retirement System (CSRS) benefits, state government benefits, military personnel benefits, etc. These benefits may provide death payments, burial expenses, pension income, health benefits, education assistance, loans, and more.

This is a lot of information, but gathering it in advance will save you time and frustration during the interview.

THE LIFE INSURANCE CLAIMS PROCESS

Although it may seem a bit uncomfortable to collect life insurance from the death of your loved one, it's a necessary action. Life insurance sometimes provides you with your single biggest financial benefit. Depending on the benefit amount, it may determine whether you must sell your home, go back to work, or can count on financial security.

To find out how much life insurance was in force and how to process it, it's always best to contact the "servicing agent" of the policy. This is typically your financial advisor or insurance agent. You can double-check by looking on a recent insurance statement.

There could be other polices too. So also check with the following sources:

- Decedent's recent and previous employers

- Your employer, for any spousal life insurance

- Decedent's bank statements for the last three years, to see if any life insurance premiums were paid

- Lenders for mortgages, personal loans, or credit cards

Many social organizations, professional associations, and unions may also offer group life insurance plans for members that provide special benefits for surviving spouses. For example, if the deceased was a member of a teacher's union, it may be possible they owned a group life insurance policy.

Even for a year afterward, continue to check the mail for any premium due notices and check with the state's unclaimed property office to see if money from life insurance policies may have been turned over to the state.

If the decedent owned life insurance but the policy can't be located or the agent's name is lost, you have a few options:

- Contact the American Council of Life Insurers (Policy Search, ACLI) and inquire about their service, "My Insurance Log." Visit www.acli.com.

- As an alternative, MIB, an insurance membership corporation, offers a policy locator service for a fee. For more information about this service, visit MIB's website at www.mib.com.

- NAIC's Life Insurance Policy Locator service is also a good tool. Currently, the URL is https://eapps.naic.org/life-policy-locator.

Ways of Receiving Life Insurance Benefits

After this discovery process, carefully evaluate the different ways you can receive your benefits:

- **Lump sum**—the entire death benefit in one check.

- **Specific income provision**—the life insurance company will pay principal and interest on a predetermined schedule.

- **Life income option**—you are guaranteed income for the duration of your life. The income amount will depend on the policy's death benefit and your age.

- **Interest income option**—the life insurance company will hold the proceeds of the policy and pay the interest earned. If you choose this option, the policy's death benefit will remain intact and be paid to your children or a secondary beneficiary upon your death.

Lastly, take the time now to review and update the beneficiaries named on your life insurance policies (and IRAs), especially if the deceased was one of your beneficiaries.

Next Steps in the Insurance Claim Process

For group policies, follow the instructions given to you by the governing organization. For personally owned life insurance, contact the company whose name and address appears on the policy, your insurance agent, or call the company's local office.

If you're listed as the beneficiary on the policy, order a claim form and prepare a claim package. Normally, your agent will help you do this; however, if you don't have an agent, here's a sample letter you can use:

[TODAY'S DATE]

ABC Insurance Company
123 Main Street
Smithville, OH 12345

Re: Policy number [YOUR POLICY NUMBER]

Dear Claims Agent,

I would like to apply for the life insurance benefits on the policy referenced above. Please send me the necessary forms and instructions to expedite this process as efficiently as possible.

Your correspondence can be sent to:

[YOUR NAME]
[YOUR MAILING ADDRESS]

If you have any questions, please contact me at [YOUR PHONE NUMBER].

Sincerely,

[SIGNATURE]

[YOUR NAME]

When you receive the paperwork, you may need:

- A certified copy of the death certificate

- The insurance policy number

- The amount listed as the death benefit or face value

- The decedent's occupation and last day of work

- The decedent's birth certificate (or other birth documentation) and your own birth certificate, depending on how you want the proceeds to be paid

Insurance companies may also request information about the circumstances of the decedent's death, including:

- Attending physician's statement

- Coroner's report

- Police incident report

- The beneficiary's age, address, and Social Security number for federal government filings

Tax Treatment of Insurance Proceeds

Life insurance proceeds are generally not considered to be taxable income to the beneficiary. However, in some cases the insurance proceeds could incur estate taxes. There are also some other conditions where life insurance could be taxed, for example, life insurance within an IRA or pension plan or a policy that had some kind of transfer for value transaction. In addition, some wills provide that any share of estate tax related to insurance proceeds should be paid from those proceeds. Check with a qualified accountant to determine if your proceeds are taxable.

Regardless of your situation, request IRS Form 712 from the insurance company at the same time the claim for the proceeds is filed. You may need it depending upon the circumstances under which your estate must file an estate tax return. Ask your attorney for more information.

EMPLOYEE BENEFITS

Contact current and all former employers of the decedent to collect the full amount of all employee benefits due to you. This is one step that many people often forget to follow through on, but you may be eligible to receive:

- The decedent's unpaid salary
- Accrued vacation and sick pay
- Workers' compensation benefits

DETERMINE RETIREMENT BENEFITS

A beneficiary can fall into one of the following categories: spouse, non-spouse, or entity, such as a trust. Depending upon what type of beneficiary you are, the Internal Revenue Service will often dictate your options.

To better understand your distribution options for IRA accounts, please refer to Chapter 7: Understand Your IRA Distribution Options. Also be sure to talk with a financial advisor and review your options thoroughly.

ASSESS HEALTH INSURANCE OPTIONS

If your spouse is the decedent, one of the biggest financial worries you may have is how to maintain your health insurance.

COBRA

If you received health insurance through your spouse's employer and are a survivor, you are likely to be eligible for health coverage through COBRA (Consolidated Omnibus Budget Reconciliation Act of 1985). COBRA covers the deceased's enrolled eligible family members for up to thirty-six months (more than the standard COBRA eighteen-month period) after their death, as long as your spouse was employed at the time of death and was covered by the company's health insurance plan. Also, in most cases, the dependent spouse must notify the health plan administrator within sixty days after the death of the covered employee.

Survivors must still pay the premiums for the plan but won't have to find, qualify for, or pay for a new health insurance plan right away.

Under COBRA, you'll be required to pay the full cost of the insurance plus a 2 percent administrative fee. In cases where the employer was paying a good portion of the monthly premium, the rate you may have to pay under COBRA will likely change.

For COBRA appeals information or notification rights, you should contact the U.S. Department of Labor Pension and Welfare Benefits Administration Division of Technical Assistance and Inquiries, 200 Constitution Ave., NW (Room N-5658), Washington, D.C. 20210 or call 866-487-2365 or (TTY: 877-889-5627).

Affordable Care Act Health Insurance

At the time of this writing, an individual can also purchase health insurance through the Affordable Care Act.

This law put in place comprehensive health insurance reforms that allow people who don't have health insurance or don't have adequate coverage to purchase it directly through an insurance marketplace.

Open enrollment for each year is from Nov. 1 of the prior year to Jan. 31 of the next year. However, if you've had certain life events, such as losing health insurance coverage, marriage, moving, having a baby, or adopting a child, you have up to sixty days after that event to enroll in health insurance coverage. You can also enroll in Medicaid and the Children's Health Insurance Plan at any time of the year.

Losing health coverage due to the death of a family member is included as one of the reasons you qualify for the Special Enrollment Period and can enroll in a health insurance plan, as long as you do so within sixty days of your loss of health insurance.

You can learn more about the health insurance plans available, their costs, and other information at healthcare.gov.

Take Advantage of Flexible Spending Account Benefits

Make sure to ask the decedent's employer if there was a medical flexible spending account (FSA) or reimbursement account for the deceased. An FSA allows for the reimbursement of out-of-pocket health expenses (those not covered by health insurance) from pre-tax dollars deducted from an employee's paycheck. Therefore, an employee's taxable income will be reduced by the amount placed in the account.

If so, make sure you file a claim for any outstanding medical bills incurred by the deceased before the end of the calendar year or this money will be lost.

Flexible spending accounts are "use-it-or-lose-it" plans. This means that amount in the account at the end of the plan year can't be carried over to the next year. In some cases, the plan may provide a grace period of up to two and a half months after the end of the plan year. If so, any qualified medical expenses incurred in that period are treated as having occurred in the previous plan year and can be paid from any amounts left in the account at the end of that year. Any monies not properly withdrawn are completely lost as your employer isn't permitted to refund any part of the balance to you.

Check on Health Savings Account Balance

Check to see if the decedent had a Health Savings Account (HSA). An HSA is a medical savings account for people enrolled in a high-deductible health plan. Unlike flexible spending accounts, HSA funds roll over and accumulate year to year if they're not spent.

HSA funds can be used to pay for qualified medical expenses at any time, without federal tax liability or penalty. Withdrawals for non-medical expenses are treated similarly to IRA withdrawals, in that they can incur tax penalties if taken before retirement age and tax advantages if withdrawn after.

COLLECT VETERANS BENEFITS

The Department of Veterans Affairs (VA) offers certain benefits and services to honor deceased veterans. The benefits include reimbursement of up to $2,000 of burial expenses, a headstone or marker, burial flag, burial in a VA National Cemetery and, for eligible recipients, a Presidential Memorial Certificate. If you forgot to collect these benefits at the time of the burial, there is no time limit on claims for reimbursement of burial expenses for a service-related death. In other cases, claims must be filed within two years of the veteran's burial.

Benefits may also be available for dependents and survivors. A death pension is payable to some surviving spouses and children of deceased wartime veterans.

Additionally, the VA Civilian Health and Medical Program (CHAMPVA) shares the cost of medical services for eligible dependents and survivors of certain veterans. There are no time limits for these benefits.

Collect Survivor Benefits

Whether surviving family members are paid such benefits will depend on a number of factors, including whether the veteran died from causes connected with military service, whether he or she served in war or peacetime, and whether the discharge was honorable or not. The surviving family's financial circumstances are also a consideration.

To check on any benefits you may be eligible for, call 800-827-1000, or visit your local Veterans Administration (VA) office. If there is no local VA office, you may contact the Veterans of Foreign Wars or the American Legion, or even the American Red Cross. The VA will need a veteran's claim number (called a "C" number) or a copy of the Certificate of Discharge from military service (DD Form 214), a military service number or branch of service and dates served. In addition, a death certificate, marriage certificate(s), and birth certificates for children may be required.

TO-DO LIST

- ❏ Look into Social Security benefits.

- ❏ Start the Social Security claims process.

- ❏ Check for and collect other government benefits.

- ❏ Begin life insurance claims process.

- ❏ Collect employee benefits.

- ❏ Determine retirement benefits.

- ❏ Assess health insurance options.

- ❏ Take advantage of flex benefits.

- ❏ If applicable, collect veterans benefits.

3

GET ORGANIZED AND SORT THROUGH THE PAPERWORK

While it's common to become overwhelmed with the mountain of paperwork from insurance and mortgage companies, creditors and banks, the decedent's employer, and many other businesses and individuals, getting a system set up to deal with it all will help.

Being organized prevents you from missing deadlines or misplacing important documents amidst the upheaval that typically accompanies the loss of a loved one.

GET ORGANIZED

Resist any temptation to throw away correspondence as a way of simplifying your life. Initially, it may be difficult to decide what's important and what isn't. With time, you'll gain a better grasp of what's important and what can be discarded.

A relatively simple way to organize all the mail, documentation, and paperwork is to start a filing system. Whether you use folders or large manila envelopes in a filing cabinet or piles on the dining room table, retain these documents in a secure place and create a system for easy retrieval.

Consider using folders or piles for each type of correspondence. Use Post-It® Notes or other clear markings to indicate due dates in plain view. In short, pick a system that works for you.

Following is a list of suggested categories and documents for each folder or pile. While this system may take some time to set up, it will provide an efficient way to retain and retrieve important documents.

Some of this organization you can do as information comes in, such as credit card bills and bank statements. Other paperwork and documents will need to be retrieved from your current household filing system.

Estate Documents

- Wills, codicils, supporting memoranda
- Trust agreements
- Powers of Attorney
- Powers of Appointment

Life Insurance

- Life insurance policies

- Copy of claim forms

- IRS Form 712 (to report life insurance proceeds)

Employer Correspondence

- Benefit claim forms

- Paycheck stubs

- Benefit plan statements

Tax Information

- Copies of individual tax returns for the past three years

- Receipts for other taxes paid

- Charitable contribution receipts

- Other deductible items

Business-Related Documents

- Partnership agreements

- Joint venture agreements

- Contracts

Bank Correspondence

- Savings account statements and passbook

- Checking account statements, register, and canceled checks

Household information and documents

- Property deed

- Homeowner's insurance policy

- Appraisals

- Records and receipts for home improvements

Bills

- List of bills—paid and unpaid

- Credit Card Statements

Automobile Papers

- Title and registration

- Automobile insurance policy

Decedent's Personal Documentation

- Death certificate

- Birth certificate

- Social Security card

- Military papers

Family's Documentation

- Birth certificates

- Social Security numbers

- Marriage certificates

- Divorce agreements

- Honorable/dishonorable discharge certificates

Investment Information

- Brokerage account statements

- Money market accounts

- Certificates of deposit

- Stock and bond certificates

- Mutual funds and IRAs

- U.S. Savings bonds

- U.S. Treasury securities

All Other Assets Owned by Decedent

- Real estate

- Personal property

Get Organized and Sort Through the Paperwork

GET ACCESS TO ONLINE ACCOUNTS

As we continue to move into a digital world, more and more information is available to us online. We pay bills online, and we receive many bills, including bank and credit card statements, via email and online accounts.

Because of this, in addition to the above documentation, you'll also need to gather information on the decedent's online accounts and how to access them. Their primary email account is the easiest place to start, as that gives you information about many other accounts.

Start by checking the decedent's computers, tablets, and cell phone. If the decedent had a smart phone, they may be automatically logged into their email account, which won't require you to input the password. As email is usually accessed regularly, they may also be logged onto their account on their computer.

If you can't access their email account or don't know their password, you can ask their email provider to provide you with access. Google, for instance, will work with immediate family members to access or close the deceased's email account. However, email providers are primarily concerned with keeping account information private and secure, rather than helping you have access to it.

If you can get access to the decedent's email account, don't delete it immediately. They may continue to receive emails about recurring bills, such as Netflix, and receive notifications about online statements from their bank, credit cards, and other financial institutions.

If the decedent has opted for electronic statements and bills, see if you can convert those back to paper statements, so that you will be able to keep track of them more easily.

However, because state and federal laws are unclear on the breadth of laws such as the Computer Fraud and Abuse Act, making it illegal to share passwords or access another person's online account, proceed with caution. While the Department of Justice has little interest in prosecuting bereaved family members trying to access their deceased loved one's electricity statement, if you feel unsure or uncertain, please consult with your attorney.

Get Organized and Sort Through the Paperwork

TO-DO LIST

- ❏ Set up a filing system.

- ❏ Collect estate-related documents.

- ❏ Collect life insurance policies and claims forms.

- ❏ Collect employer benefits paperwork and claims forms.

- ❏ Find last three years of tax returns and receipts.

- ❏ Collect business-related agreements and contracts.

- ❏ Assemble bank statements, canceled checks, and register.

- ❏ Put together house-related papers.

- ❏ Collect paid and unpaid bills and credit card statements.

- ❏ Locate automobile title, registration, and insurance policy.

- ❏ Locate decedent's personal documentation: birth and death certificates, Social Security card, and military papers.

- ❏ Collect personal documentation from your family.

- ❏ Locate investment and other asset documentation.

4

REVIEW ASSETS

Prior to paying any bills or distributing any money, it's a good idea to review all of the assets now available to you. This will give you a better understanding of what you have to work with and what needs to be addressed.

On the surface, the decedent's savings and investments may seem straightforward. However, there may be some complications that aren't obvious. For example, they might have owned bonds with maturity dates, CDs with estate clauses, investment partnerships with cash call provisions, and so on. If they owned rental property, it might have created cash flow over the years but, if the decedent didn't take care of the property properly, it may now need significant deferred maintenance.

While it's important to document all the assets, it's equally important to get a basic understanding of what they are, the rights and obligations related to the ownership of them, and if they represent a net cash inflow or outflow.

So, given the above possible complications and the possibility that the decedent's attorney may have implemented post-mortem planning techniques, make sure to seek the advice of an attorney prior to exercising any of these action items.

EVALUATE FINANCIAL ACCOUNTS

Get a handle on all of the existing checking, savings, money market, or Certificate of Deposit (CD) accounts, held individually or jointly in the decedent's name. If the decedent is your spouse, first get your attorney's approval, then discuss with representatives of each bank the possibility of switching joint accounts to an individual account in your name. If you're not sure which banks must be contacted, check the decedent's previous year's tax return. If a Schedule B was filed with the tax return, you may be able to obtain information about the pertinent institutions as they are often listed in the section titled Interest Income.

EVALUATE OPTIONS FOR RETIREMENT ACCOUNTS

If your loved one had an Individual Retirement Account (IRA) and you are named as the beneficiary, be sure to carefully explore all of your distribution options. This topic is thoroughly discussed in Chapter 7: Understand Your IRA Distribution Options.

TRANSFER STOCKS, BONDS, AND BROKERAGE ACCOUNTS

If your attorney authorizes it, contact the financial advisors at each firm to have them transfer jointly owned securities to you or the surviving owner(s). They may ask you to resend copies of the death certificate before the transfer can be made.

In some cases, your loved one may have stocks held outside of a brokerage firm. While less common nowadays, some people prefer to hold stock certificates on their own rather than with a financial advisor. Should this be the case, you'll need to contact the transfer agent listed on the stock's corresponding statement.

If you aren't sure whether the decedent has securities held outside a brokerage account, make a list of all the companies from which they received dividend checks and compare them to the list of securities held in their brokerage account. If you discover that they are, in fact, receiving checks from additional companies, contact each company's investor relations department.

CHECK ON CURRENT MORTGAGES AND NOTES RECEIVABLE

Check to see if the decedent held any mortgages on residential or commercial property or held notes on automobiles or other personal property that was sold to individuals or businesses.

There may also be outstanding personal loans for which payments are due. All of these assets are considered part of the estate. Make sure the monthly payments are directed to the appropriate person or persons as determined by the will or executor of the estate.

If the deceased held debt at JP Morgan Chase and was killed in combat action or died in a combat theater of operations since January 1, 2011, they may be granted debt relief through the bank's unique Military Survivor Program. If a service member was liable for debt, the balances may be canceled for most existing Chase mortgages, auto loans, credit cards, student loans, and other consumer or business debt. For specific criteria and eligibility requirements, call Chase Military Services at 877-469-0110 or if overseas: 1-318-340-3308 (collect). They also accept operator relay calls. If you're deaf, hard of hearing, or have a speech disability, call 711 for assistance.

CHECK THE TITLE FOR REAL ESTATE

If your home was held in joint name, the title doesn't necessarily need to be changed. The property may automatically become the property of the surviving owner. If the real estate was in the sole name of the deceased, then the title must be changed to list the beneficiaries' name(s) as the new owner(s). This is done as part of the probate process.

KEEP OR CASH OUT ANNUITIES

Check any fixed or variable deferred annuities held in the decedent's name to determine the amount of the death benefit due to you or other survivors. In some instances, beneficiaries may be entitled to an "enhanced death benefit" that is based upon the policy's highest anniversary value or other predetermined formula. Additionally, some annuities have "income riders" that allow beneficiaries to receive a guaranteed stream of income, rather than a lump sum. It's important to understand these potential benefits. Make sure to speak with your financial advisor or insurance agent for details. Also, consult with an accountant or tax professional to consider the tax ramifications when deciding whether to keep or cash out the annuity.

TRANSFER OWNERSHIP OF AUTOMOBILES, BOATS, AND VEHICLES

Remember, by law, a member of the immediate family of the deceased owner may continue to use the vehicle until the registration or insurance expires. Eventually, when it comes time to change ownership of the vehicle, you'll need to establish its value—this will dictate your next step.

Refer to Chapter 8: Attend to Personal Affairs for more information about how to go about transferring ownership of vehicles.

DIGITAL ASSETS

Dealing with digital assets after death is a new phenomenon that still holds a lot of unknowns, in terms of the ability and legality of accessing online accounts and how to assess the value of certain digital assets.

More and more of our life is lived online. We store everything from email and photos to tax information online. However, due to a mix of sometimes contradictory online user agreements, state laws, and federal laws, there is no clear-cut answer as to how to take control of or even get access to the decedent's online accounts. As time passes, more and more states are beginning to tackle the issue and draft legislation to give clear guidelines on dealing with digital assets.

New York, for instance, has proposed legislation that provides the estate executor or administrator access to a decedent's email, social networking, and blogging accounts.

Most people's digital assets will have sentimental value, rather than financial value—their online photo albums, emails to relatives and friends, or social media posts, for instance. Often, a local copy of these will exist on their computer or smart phone or can be downloaded from social media sites such as Facebook. More guidance on social media is provided in Chapter 8: Attend to Personal Affairs.

However, there are digital assets that do have financial value to consider, such as libraries of digital music, movies, and games.

Review Assets

Other assets, such as an income-earning website or internet domain name should also be considered. Should anything like this pertain to you, talk with your attorney for more information.

TO-DO LIST

- ☐ Evaluate existing financial accounts.
- ☐ Switch joint bank accounts to individual accounts.
- ☐ Transfer jointly owned securities to beneficiaries.
- ☐ Locate any stock certificates held by decedent.
- ☐ Evaluate retirement accounts.
- ☐ Check on any current mortgages and notes receivable.
- ☐ Locate the title for all real estate holdings.
- ☐ Evaluate whether to keep or cash out annuities.
- ☐ Evaluate digital assets.

5

PAY THE BILLS

Mounting bills may cause you anxiety, but there are definite rules for how and when to pay bills held in the sole name of the decedent. This chapter will help you sort through the pile, pay appropriate bills, and conserve the assets of the estate.

First, don't be in a rush to pay off the decedent's bills. And, although you might feel like you're being helpful, you may not want to pay off the decedent's debts from your own funds. The estate is responsible for satisfying the debts of the decedent, and the available funds should go first to pay for funeral expenses, then attorneys, and, lastly, creditors. In other words, if the estate runs out of money before the creditors (including hospitals) get paid, you may not have to pay them. Bottom line: consult with your attorney before paying any bills.

PAY FUNERAL EXPENSES

Funeral expenses may be deductible from the decedent's federal estate tax return, so make sure you keep proof of payment for all the expenses, including those for the funeral director, burial plot, headstone, or cremation.

INQUIRE WITH CREDITORS

Contact all creditors and see if there was any life insurance tied to the loans, mortgages, or credit cards. It's not common, but sometimes people will elect for insurance at the time the loan was taken and then later forget about it. Should this be the case, the deceased may have carried life insurance on those borrowings and the entire balance due may be paid off by the policy.

Just inquire, though. Do not yet pay off any balances. For more details on how to proceed, see Chapter 6: Process and Manage the Estate for more information.

TERMINATE VEHICLE LEASES

In many cases, death is considered "early termination" of the lease contract, which can mean thousands of dollars in penalty fees. Sometimes, however, there is hope. Some leasing companies allow a lease obligation to be forgiven upon the death of the lessee. If the decedent was leasing their vehicle and you don't want to keep it, see if the lease has a death clause. If so, you may be able to get out of the lease at no cost and simply return the vehicle.

Ford Credit, for example, has a program called Peace of Mind, which allows customers who are sixty-two years of age or older to lease or finance a new vehicle without the worry of creating a future financial burden for their families. Peace of Mind provides options designed to enable a family or estate to adjust in the event a customer should pass away before completing the lease or finance contract—at no extra cost. These options include the opportunity to keep the vehicle or to turn it in and be freed of the remaining contractual obligations.

Similarly, under Mercedes's Customer Bereavement Program, the family can choose to return the leased vehicle within ten days of death and owe nothing further. If the family decides to keep leasing the vehicle and the new lessee meets credit criteria, no transfer fee is charged.

If you don't discover a death clause, you may still have some protection because the lease remains a liability of the estate, not the survivor, so long as you didn't sign or cosign the lease.

TERMINATE CELL PHONE CONTRACTS

To cancel or transfer a cell phone contract, call your provider's customer support number. Tell the representative that you'd like to cancel or transfer the contract and the reason why. Canceling or transferring a contract after death is often free.

Expect to provide them with the deceased's date of death and Social Security number. Some companies may need a certified copy of the death certificate.

If the deceased had a desirable phone number, consider whether you or another family member would like to keep the phone number.

TRANSFER MORTGAGES AND NOTES PAYABLE

Generally speaking, mortgages and notes payable follow the asset to which they are attached. So, whoever is awarded ownership of the decedent's property will be responsible for satisfying the corresponding mortgage or lien against it. That said, you will not have to requalify for the mortgage. As long as you have title to the home, the Garn-St. Germain Depository Institutions Act of 1982 prohibits lenders from calling in their deceased borrowers' mortgages. When you talk with the bank, also be sure to check on any possible mortgage insurance benefits.

CLOSE ONLINE ACCOUNTS

If the decedent had accounts with online retailers or held any web-based subscriptions, you should consider either closing or updating these online accounts with the proper user and billing/shipping information, if you're able to do so under the account's terms of service agreement.

MEET CHARITABLE PLEDGES

It's an ethical obligation to make good on any outstanding pledges to charities. Review the decedent's checking account for the past two years and look for donations sent to charities. This will help you identify those charities that the decedent supported through annual giving programs.

MANAGE INCOME TAXES

A surviving spouse may file a joint tax return for the tax year in which the death occurred. However, if the surviving spouse remarried before the end of the year, the filing status of the decedent should be married filing separately.

A surviving spouse with dependent children may be eligible to use Qualifying Widow(er) with Dependent Child as the filing status for two years following the year of death of their spouse. For example, if the spouse died in 2022, and the survivor doesn't remarry, they may be able to use this filing status for both the 2023 and 2024 tax years as well.

This filing status entitles you to use joint return tax rates and the highest standard deduction amount if you don't itemize deductions. This status doesn't entitle you to file a joint return.

The surviving spouse is eligible to file their tax return as a Qualifying Widow(er) with Dependent Child if they meet all of the following:

- The surviving spouse was entitled to file a joint return with their spouse for the year their spouse died. It doesn't matter whether a joint return was actually filed.

- The surviving spouse didn't remarry before the end of the tax year in which the decedent died.

- The spouse has a child, stepchild, or adopted child for whom they can claim an exemption. This doesn't include a foster child.

- The surviving spouse paid more than half the cost of keeping up a home that is the main home for themselves and their child for the entire year, except for temporary absences.

- The child lived with you in your home all year, except for temporary absences.

The IRS booklet Publication 559, *Information for Survivors, Executors, and Administrators,* may be helpful. You can order a copy of this publication by going online to www.irs.gov or by calling the IRS Forms Distribution Center at 800-829-3676. As with all tax matters, it's best to consult with your accountant or tax professional before taking any action.

PAY ESTATE TAXES

Generally speaking, if a federal estate tax return must be filed, taxes are due within nine months of the date of death. However, there are conditions under which an estate can ask for an extension of time to pay death taxes. In those cases where the government grants an extension, the estate will pay interest on the amount of unpaid taxes. An attorney or accountant can help you navigate through those waters. If the estate tax isn't paid within nine months and an extension hasn't been granted, you'll owe substantial interest and penalties.

Legislation surrounding estate tax continues to change. As of 2022, the estate and gift tax limits for an individual were at $12.06 million. This means that for a person dying in 2022, no federal estate tax will be imposed if his or her gross estate is less than $12.06 million. Double this for married people. While this big number means that most estates won't be taxable, it's important not to assume that any particular estate is not. Because tax laws frequently change, you'll need to contact an accountant or tax attorney to understand your options and determine the most beneficial course of action.

DEATH'S RED TAPE

TO-DO LIST

- ❏ Pay funeral expenses and retain receipts.

- ❏ Consult with your attorney before paying other bills.

- ❏ Notify creditors of the death.

- ❏ Check to see if there was life insurance on any loans, mortgages, and credit cards.

- ❏ Terminate vehicle lease and/or see if there was a death clause on the car lease.

- ❏ Cancel cell phone contracts.

- ❏ Transfer mortgages and notes to new owners.

- ❏ Close accounts with online retailers, cancel online subscriptions, etc.

- ❏ Meet charitable obligations.

- ❏ Determine filing status for income tax returns.

- ❏ File federal estate tax returns within nine months.

6

PROCESS AND MANAGE THE ESTATE

ONCE YOU HAVE ALL THE ASSETS CALCULATED AND THE OUTSTANDING bills are under control, finalizing the decedent's estate is your next concern.

There are different types of estates, such as those established by a will, or by the probate court if there wasn't a will. There are also living trusts, set up by the decedent before their death, which are addressed at the end of this chapter.

UNDERSTAND YOUR ROLE AS EXECUTOR

The executor, personal representative, or administrator is the person who carries out the responsibility of finalizing the estate. An executor (or executrix) is appointed by the decedent in their will. An administrator is appointed by the probate court if the decedent didn't name an executor, didn't have a will, or the person named in the will isn't able or willing to fulfill the role, and has the same responsibilities as the executor. In many cases, this person is the surviving spouse but can also be another family member or close family friend.

The executor is responsible for administering and distributing the decedent's property and carrying out the wishes specified in the will. An executor's role varies from state to state. In general, they are charged with listing the assets of the decedent's estate, collecting money owed to it, and paying the estate's debts (see Chapter 5: Pay the Bills). Executors are also responsible for disbursing property to the appropriate beneficiaries. A decedent's will may also specifically authorize other responsibilities or powers.

While it's recommended and often common practice to hire an attorney for advice in settling the estate, it's not mandatory. If the estate is small and uncomplicated, it may be possible to handle the estate administration without hiring an attorney. In New York, for example, estates with assets below a certain value that don't contain real estate can be processed through Surrogate's Court for a minimal filing fee of one dollar.

GATHER ALL SIGNIFICANT DOCUMENTS

The person managing the decedent's affairs bears the ultimate responsibility for gathering and retaining the decedent's key documents, including:

- The original will and any subsequent revised wills or codicils

- Trust agreements

- Power of attorney (POA)

- Note: In some states, certain instructions in a healthcare power of attorney may need to be carried out after the decedent's death. While most powers of attorney cease to be valid after an individual's death, you may still want to gather those documents and make sure that all institutions know that the agent named in the power of attorney no longer has any legal authority to transact business on behalf of the decedent

- The decedent's birth certificate

- The decedent's Social Security card

- Check register

- Savings and certificate of deposit account passbooks

- Stock and bond certificates

- Insurance policies

- Real property deeds and titles

- Personal property titles

- Marriage and divorce certificates

- Military papers

- Certified death certificates to file claims for life insurance, survivor benefits, and to change the title of property and financial accounts

If you're unable to locate originals or certified copies of marriage or birth certificates, divorce agreements, military service papers, or Social Security cards, check with your local Department of Vital Records.

ESTABLISH CRITICAL RECORDS

Keep an organized list of all property, income, debts, and expenses of the estate. This documentation will prove useful when closing the estate. See Chapter 3: Get Organized and Sort Through the Paperwork for more information.

INVENTORY THE ASSETS

Make a list of the assets of the estate. This includes all real and personal property as well as the titles and/or deeds for each asset.

SUBMIT THE WILL TO PROBATE

Probate is the legal process used to prove the validity of a written will. To begin, contact the clerk of the probate court (sometimes also referred to as the Surrogate's Court or Register or Registry of Wills) in the deceased's county for the necessary procedures. (In some cases, the deceased may have lived in one county and the executor in another.) It is important to authorize distribution of property according to the will's specific provisions. If you need to probate the will, you may need to hire an attorney to assist you. It's not necessary to use the same attorney who drafted the will.

Once the will is filed with the probate court, the court will formally appoint the executor named in the will and issue Letters Testamentary, which authorize the executor to begin settlement procedures. The executor is also responsible for collecting monies owed to the decedent, paying the decedent's debts, managing and distributing the property, and submitting a final accounting to the court.

When an individual dies without a will, the process of distributing a decedent's estate is known as estate administration. Each state has laws of descent that dictate the distribution of an estate if there is no valid will. These laws usually provide for the surviving spouse, children, or close relatives to receive shares of the estate.

The first step is to have the court issue Letters of Administration authorizing the appointed administrator to settle the estate.

UNFREEZE NEEDED ASSETS

Until the probate process is completed, bank accounts and other assets may be frozen, safe-deposit boxes sealed, and other steps taken to protect the interests of heirs and to conserve assets subject to estate taxes and debts. Sometimes, exceptions are made. For example, banks will often allow a surviving spouse to withdraw funds to meet daily living expenses until the estate is settled. Should the bank refuse to allow any assets to be withdrawn, the court can order the release of assets from the estate.

CHECK ASSETS NOT SUBJECT TO PROBATE

Certain assets aren't subject to probate because they're held in ways that result in the passing of ownership directly to an intended beneficiary upon the death of the owner without going through any probate process.

One of the most common non-probate assets is a home held by spouses jointly with a right of survivorship. The property automatically becomes the sole property of the surviving owner upon the death of the decedent.

Individuals may also own bank or brokerage accounts with a "right of survivorship" or another form of ownership known as "payable on death" or "transfer on death" registration. In states that recognize POD and TOD arrangements, such bank or brokerage accounts will transfer as quickly and easily as if they had been owned with a right of survivorship.

The other widely owned class of assets that can be transferred at death without probate court involvement are assets such as life insurance and retirement accounts. These assets may pass under the terms of an individual's will but usually only if the individual names their estate as the beneficiary. Otherwise, life insurance proceeds and monies from retirement accounts will be paid directly to the named beneficiary.

CONTACT HEIRS AND BENEFICIARIES

Follow through to make sure the attorney and/or the court notifies all persons who are named in the will and likely to receive assets from the estate. Retain a list of their names, addresses, birth dates, Social Security numbers, and telephone numbers for paperwork and such.

Some state laws require the decedent's personal representative to publish a death notice in their local paper. The death notice serves as a public notice of the estate's probate and enables people who think they have an interest in the estate (such as creditors) to file a claim against the estate within a specified time period.

ESTABLISH AN ESTATE ACCOUNT

When necessary (either required by the court procedural rules or your bank or due to the sheer volume of assets and/or beneficiaries), the executor will open an estate checking account. The estate checking account is used to combine all the decedent's liquid assets and pay the expenses of the estate.

To open an estate checking account, the executor (or your attorney) may need to obtain an Employer Identification number (EIN), similar to an individual Social Security number. An EIN can only be obtained through the IRS. There's no fee for an EIN, and the online application is simple. Go to https://www.irs.gov/businesses/small-businesses-self-employed/apply-for-an-employer-identification-number-ein-online or go to www.irs.gov and search for "EIN." Be careful of third parties who offer to do this for you for free or for a nominal fee. Alternatively, you can call the IRS. Either way, before obtaining an EIN, you should consult your attorney.

ENSURE THAT PROPERTY IS PROPERLY INSURED

Insurance policies that protect the real and personal property held by the estate, including fire, theft, casualty, and collision insurance, should be maintained and even improved if necessary. Be sure to notify the various insurance carriers of any changes in coverage. Furthermore, depending on state probate procedures, the executor or administrator may be required to obtain a bond before Letters Testamentary/Administration are issued.

TAKE CAUTION WHEN CHANGING NAMES ON ACCOUNTS

Before making any name changes on accounts or claiming assets by beneficiary designation, be sure to check with your attorney, as your own estate plan may be adversely affected. A simple name change or even cashing a check payable in joint name or solely to the decedent can abolish the opportunity for certain postmortem plans, such as the process of disclaiming assets.

If it's appropriate to change the names on bank accounts, mutual funds, stock, and other financial accounts, bring a copy of the death certificate to each financial institution. Stocks or bonds bequeathed to particular people or entities by the decedent's will must be reregistered in the beneficiaries' names.

The title to real estate may also need to be updated to reflect the change in ownership.

COLLECT OUTSTANDING RECEIVABLES

All debts owed to the decedent or the estate may be collected now or may need to have payments redirected to the estate. Either way, these are among the assets that comprise the estate.

Collect unpaid receivables such as salary, insurance, and employee benefits. Review the deceased's personal records to ensure that the estate receives all benefits due from his or her employer and any insurance companies. Contact the benefits office of both current and past employers for more information. See Chapter 2: Collect Survivor Benefits for more information.

VALUE THE ASSETS

One reason to value the estate is if it's anticipated to be over the estate tax exemption, which varies from state to state. The federal exemption in 2017 was $5.49 million per individual ($10.98 million for a married couple). That means if an individual leaves more than $5.49 million to heirs, they will likely owe federal estate tax.

Regardless of the estate size, if the estate has multiple beneficiaries, then the estate and its contents should be appraised as of the date of death (or alternative date). This way it can be divvied up according to the deceased's wishes.

While valuations are commonly done as of the date of death, you might also try to project the value of such assets in the future, say six to twelve months from that date. Highly collectible items, such as sports memorabilia, artwork, and other possessions, may naturally increase in value over time or may have their value tied to a key event such as a sports record or the death of the artist. Anticipating any change to the value of each item—either higher or lower—will help you make better, more informed decisions. For the more valuable or unique possessions, you may consider hiring an appraiser to value the item for public sale.

If there are a tremendous number of items in the collection, the family or beneficiaries may consider donating the entire collection to a museum or not-for-profit organization. You could also consider holding an auction or estate sale or trying your hand at an online auction. Online auction sites, such as eBay, often require a photo, brief description, and a minimum price you'd be willing to accept. Once the sale has been made, you're responsible for packing and shipping the item to the buyer. If you're reluctant to handle the online auction yourself, you should consider hiring a third-party asset liquidator. They are often very helpful and a minimal cost. At most, be prepared to pay 30 to 50 percent of the final purchase price as a commission.

NOTIFY CREDITORS AND PAY BILLS

Notify all creditors in writing of the decedent's passing. Prior to paying outstanding debts, consult an attorney since only those debts incurred by the decedent alone are considered debts of the estate.

In cases where there are no probate assets, the estate is said to be insolvent; therefore, any outstanding debts may not be able to be satisfied. Furthermore, families have no personal responsibilities for the decedent's debts. Keep in mind that paying debts, such as funeral expenses, attorney's fees, estate administration expenses, and various taxes, are given priority by the state.

Also note that for those decedents living in a community property state, a spouse is considered liable for any marital debt, even if the debt was solely incurred by the decedent. Consult an attorney for clarification on these issues and before paying any debts.

DETERMINE FEDERAL AND STATE ESTATE TAX LIABILITY

Calculate the total value of the gross estate and compare it to the current IRS exemption. Note that the gross estate is different than the probate estate. Often, the gross estate will include life insurance proceeds even though they are payable directly to beneficiaries, other assets with designated beneficiaries, and jointly owned property with a right of survivorship. Note that some states have inheritance tax paid not by the estate but by the recipient of estate assets.

FILE FEDERAL AND STATE ESTATE TAX RETURNS

If the gross estate is larger than the current exemption, a federal estate tax return must be filed *within nine months after the decedent's death*. The IRS requires the executor or administrator of the estate to file Federal Estate Tax Form 706. If you need additional time to complete the estate tax return, you can file Form 4768 on or before the due date requesting a six-month extension of time to file the return.

Note: The extension only extends the time to file the return, not the time to pay any estate tax if there is tax due.

Also, ask your attorney or tax preparer if there is a state filing requirement that must also be fulfilled. Each state has its own timeline and forms.

DETERMINE FEDERAL AND STATE ESTATE INCOME TAX LIABILITY

This is different from the overall estate tax. The estate can earn income, which must also have taxes paid on it. Gross income includes dividends, interest, rents, royalties, capital gains, and income from businesses, partnerships, trusts, and other sources. If the estate has a gross income of $600 or more during a taxable year, the IRS requires the executor or administrator to file form 1041, U.S. Income Tax Return for Estates and Trusts. This return would segregate income earned before the date of death and income earned after the date of death. Again, ask your attorney or tax preparer if there is also a state requirement.

DISTRIBUTE ASSETS

Consult with appropriate heirs and beneficiaries about the orderly distribution of estate assets. Generally, executors may not distribute the estate assets until after the period for creditors to make claims expires, which can be as long as one year after the death.

BE AWARE OF DISCLAIMERS

Consider possible disclaimers of beneficial or joint interests by the surviving spouse or other beneficiaries. Some beneficiaries may disclaim amounts that they may be owed from the estate. This means that they refuse to accept the gift for a variety of reasons. When a beneficiary disclaims a gift, it goes to the next contingent beneficiary. This can be done to avoid credit claims or taxes, or for other reasons.

This option should be considered early in the process to preserve the beneficiary's ability to disclaim.

PREPARE AND DISTRIBUTE A FINAL REPORT TO THE BENEFICIARIES

The executor needs to create an account of their actions (assets collected and debts and expenses paid) and then ask the beneficiaries to release them from any liability to them. As executor, it helps to know about this up front because you may want to be organized in your record keeping from the start of the process.

PROCESSING A LIVING TRUST

If the deceased had a living trust, the estate settlement will be different from that of someone who had a traditional will. A living trust, properly called a revocable inter vivos trust, is often used in conjunction with a will to avoid either probate in the event of death or to establish guardianship in the event of incapacitation.

At the death of the grantor—the person who funded the trust—the living trust becomes irrevocable and the named assets are distributed according to the terms of the trust. Title transfers upon death generally are easier with trust assets than assets titled in the decedent's name alone, since typically the survivor simply needs to produce a copy of the death certificate and trust document to transfer property. Thus, in many cases, distribution of assets from a trust doesn't require court supervision (i.e., no probate). An exception would be if the decedent had a "pour-over" provision in the will directing any assets that are not titled to the trust be put into the trust at his or her death. These assets will still be subject to probate and directed to the trust by a decedent's will.

Whether probated or not, assets of the living trust are still included in the value of the estate for purposes of estate income and inheritance tax.

Nonetheless, trusts are an excellent tool for proper management and distribution of assets. In addition, trusts usually don't become a "public document," thus providing privacy to your family.

The following checklist found in this chapter may not cover every responsibility. To properly complete the entire estate process, the executor and survivor should always work closely with an attorney.

TO-DO LIST

- ❏ Ensure an executor or administrator is named.

- ❏ Gather all significant documents of the decedent.

- ❏ Keep an organized list of all property, income, debts, and expenses of the estate.

- ❏ Inventory the estate's assets.

- ❏ Contact the clerk of the probate court to process the estate.

- ❏ Obtain a bond before Letters Testamentary or Administration are issued (if needed).

- ❏ Unfreeze needed assets.

- ❏ Contact all heirs and beneficiaries.

- ❏ Obtain an Employer Identification Number (EIN) and establish a bank account for the estate (if needed).

- ❏ Ensure that all real and personal property owned by the estate is fully insured.

- ❏ Collect all debts owed to the estate or have payments redirected to the estate.

Process and Manage the Estate

❑ Inventory and value the high-ticket items and make a decision whether to liquidate and when.

❑ Notify all known creditors in writing and place a death notice to see if any additional creditors come forward.

❑ File state and federal tax returns within nine months.

❑ Distribute assets, ensuring there are adequate funds retained to cover taxes or closing costs.

❑ Process the living trust, if applicable.

7

UNDERSTAND YOUR IRA DISTRIBUTION OPTIONS

DECIDING WHAT TO DO WITH AN INHERITED IRA IS AMONG THE MOST important and complex decisions you'll face. After all, choosing the right strategy will determine how much you receive over what period and how much is paid in income tax. So, let's carefully review the options you'll want to ponder.

RULES, RULES, RULES

As part of a larger government spending package signed into law in December 2019, Congress included reforms to make saving for retirement easier for many Americans. The Setting Every Community Up for Retirement Enhancement (SECURE) Act introduced several material changes aimed at helping people save more for retirement. Unfortunately, the changes were not good for beneficiaries. The new regulation includes unfavorable tax treatment for heirs, and the various ways you can receive the money can be confusing.

The distribution options available to you depend on three factors: if you are a spouse or non-spouse, if you are at least fifty-nine-and-a-half, and if the account owner died before or after age seventy-two. Answering these questions is easy, but each scenario has its own set of options and it's essential you make the right choice. If you choose wrong, the financial implications and tax consequences could be significant.

First, you must determine your relationship to the original account owner. The IRS classifies an eligible designated beneficiary (EDB) as either:

- The owner's surviving spouse

- The owner's child who is less than eighteen years of age

- A disabled individual

- A chronically ill individual

- Any other individual who is not more than ten years younger than the deceased IRA owner

Next, you will evaluate the options available to you. Presuming the original IRA owner died on or after January 1, 2020, there are four possible distribution options. The availability of each depends on your relationship to the deceased:

- Treat as your own

- Inherited IRA depleted within ten years

- Inherited IRA depleted over your lifetime

- Disclaim the IRA

GET EXPERT ADVICE

Making the right choice involves a good understanding of your taxes, cash flow needs, goals, etc. So, I recommend seeking the counsel of a CERTIFIED FINANCIAL PLANNER™ professional or Certified Public Accountant. They will help you make an informed decision and, if needed, adjust other facets of your financial plan.

It is also crucial to speak with your estate planning attorney. The estate plan might be designed around the expectation that you "disclaim the IRA." Not a common tactic, but if it was planned for and inadvertently circumvented, there could be serious financial repercussions.

TO-DO LIST

- ❑ Determine your relationship to the original account owner.

- ❑ With the help of an expert, determine which of the options are best for you.

- ❑ Check with your attorney to make sure you shouldn't disclaim the IRA money.

- ❑ Complete forms to initiate proper distributions.

8

ATTEND TO PERSONAL AFFAIRS

Tending to your deceased loved one's personal affairs can be quite emotional. There's something about the finality of these simple tasks that makes them daunting. With that in mind, you may want to delegate some of the following tasks to trusted friends or family.

DECIDE WHAT TO DO WITH PERSONAL BELONGINGS

After sorting through their personal possessions and distributing meaningful items to family and friends, it's time to look at other avenues for putting your loved one's remaining possessions to good use.

Start by sorting items into three piles: items you want to keep, items you can let go of, and items you're not yet sure what to do with. Then, put away the items you wish to keep, donate or sell the items you can let go of, and set aside the remaining pile for later. Repeat this process if necessary.

One of the nicest ways to honor your loved one's life is to donate their belongings so they can make a difference for others. Coats, clothes, eyeglasses, shoes and boots, games, vehicles, etc. can all be donated to worthy causes.

Start by choosing charities that your loved one might have had an affinity with and then add others that would have also appealed to them. There are also charities with specific programs that may appeal to you. For example, the Lion's Club is always looking for used eyeglasses to repair and distribute to needy individuals.

Dress for Success (www.dressforsuccess.org) and Career Gear (www.careergear.org) are not-for-profit organizations that operate an impressive clothing exchange to help low-income women and men, respectively, suit up for job interviews and be positioned for success. If you're affiliated with a church or temple that has a secondhand store, donation is a wonderful way to support their ongoing community outreach programs. Your local United Way can also give you a comprehensive list of charities in your area.

In order for the beneficiary to receive a tax deduction for the contribution of the deceased's clothing, they must estimate the value of each item. Check for the original sales receipts or credit card receipts, if available, to gauge the value. This is especially important for more expensive items. Refer to IRS Publication 561,

Determining the Value of Donated Property. The fair market value is often about 30 percent of the item's original price, as long as it is in good condition.

DECIDE WHAT TO DO WITH EXCESS MEDICAL EQUIPMENT AND SUPPLIES

If this death occurred after a long illness, chances are your house is filled with a wide variety of half-empty prescription bottles, unused medical supplies, and medical equipment. The longer these items remain in your home, the longer you may be reminded of your loved one's struggle to survive. Consider putting these items to good use by donating them.

Medical equipment can often be donated to your local volunteer ambulance corps, who will provide it to citizens of your town free of charge. Local low-cost clinics also often accept medical equipment from individuals, as do the not-for-profit organizations Med-EQ and MedShare. Learn more about them online at www.med-eq.org and www.medshare.org.

If money is tight, you may also consider selling the equipment you have on eBay or other online auction sites. You'll still be making it possible for someone to purchase the equipment at a lower price.

If you have leftover prescription medicine, you have a few options. World Medical Relief accepts donations of prescription medicine.

Learn more at www.worldmedicalrelief.org. If you decide you'd prefer to dispose of the medication, rather than donate it, visit www.dea.gov to look for a Drug Enforcement Agency National Prescription Take-Back Day event or authorized collector. If you can't find one in your area, you can follow these steps from the DEA to dispose of most medicines in your household trash:

1. Mix medicines (don't crush tablets or capsules) with an unpalatable substance such as dirt, kitty litter, or used coffee grounds.

2. Place the mixture in a container such as a sealed plastic bag.

3. Throw the container in your household trash.

4. Scratch out all personal information on the prescription label of your empty pill bottle or empty medicine packaging to make it unreadable, then dispose of the container.

REDUCE SOLICITORS

Receiving mail and phone calls in your loved one's name can be a painful reminder that they're no longer here, especially when it's junk mail and solicitation calls. Here are some ways to reduce the amount of mail, email, and phone calls you receive for your deceased loved one.

Attend to Personal Affairs

Reduce Unsolicited Mail

Founded in 1917, the Direct Marketing Association is the oldest and largest national trade organization serving the direct marketing industry. To remove the decedent's name from mailing lists, magazines, catalogs, newsletters, book/music clubs, etc., visit dmachoice.org and register your deceased loved one, free of charge, on the Deceased Do Not Contact List (DDNC), which all Direct Marketing Association members are required to honor.

When you register a name with the DDNC, that person's name, address, phone number, and email address are put in a special do not contact file. A new, updated file is distributed to DMA members every three months. The service is also available to nonmembers of the DMA so that all marketers may take advantage of this service to eliminate names.

If you'd like to remove your own name, you can also do that through their website through their DMA choice program. If you prefer to do it by mail, send them a letter with the following information and a check for a few dollars payable to the Association of National Advertisers (ANA). Include the first and last names for up to three people at the same address (or three variations of your name at the same address), your street address, city, state, and zip code, and email address, so they can contact you when your three-year registration period has expired. Sign the letter and mail it to:

    DMA Choice
    Consumer Preferences
    PO Box 900
    Cos Cob, CT 06807

Stop Unsolicited Credit Card Applications

Everyone is used to getting regular solicitations from credit card companies and even preapproved credit cards from banks and finance companies. There is a very easy way to reduce both and even save some trees in the process. Now you can make a single phone call to 888-5-OPT-OUT or 888-567-8688, a toll-free number established by the credit reporting industry.

When you call this number, you can request to have your name and address removed from national credit bureau lists that are sold to the credit industry. The three national credit reporting agencies—Experian (formerly TRW), TransUnion, and Equifax—will remove your name for a five-year period from any list provided to others relating to any potential consumer credit transaction that you don't initiate. You'll have to provide some personal information and follow the directions you receive from a prerecorded message. If you follow these directions, your name should be removed within five business days.

You can also go to: https://www.optoutprescreen.com.

You can even have your name permanently removed by requesting that the credit bureau send you an "election form." This form, when filled out and returned by you, will remove your name and address from credit bureau mailing lists until you notify them that you want to be placed on these lists again.

Reduce Phone Solicitations

Is there anyone who likes getting unsolicited phone calls?

The federal government's Do Not Call Registry is a free, easy way to reduce the telemarketing calls you get at home. Visit www.donotcall.gov or call 888-382-1222 from the phone number you want to register. You'll get fewer telemarketing calls within thirty-one days of registering, and your phone number will only be removed from the registry if it's disconnected or reassigned, or if you choose to remove it from the registry yourself.

The Do Not Call Registry accepts registrations from both cell phones and land lines. There is no separate registry for cell phones.

If you receive unsolicited phone calls from telemarketers or nonprofits, the most efficient way to get them to stop calling you is to say, "Please put me on your do not call list."

Reduce Email Solicitations and Spam

Whether or not we like it, spam or unwanted email solicitations are something we've all had to learn to deal with. But you can reduce the number of unsolicited emails you and the decedent receive by opting out through the Direct Marketing Association's Email Preference Service. Visit www.dmachoice.org for more information. Adding the decedent to the DMA's Deceased Do Not Contact list should also include email solicitations.

HOW TO HANDLE EMAIL ACCOUNTS

Today, so much communication takes place over the internet that email addresses have become as significant as U.S. mailing addresses.

You may selectively use the decedent's email address book to determine names of people who should be notified of their death.

Consider keeping their email account open for several months following the death. However, due to unclear federal law in terms of the legality of using an email account other than your own, make sure you have your own email account to which you can redirect important correspondence as well as further weed out junk email and undesired web-based solicitations.

HOW TO HANDLE SOCIAL MEDIA ACCOUNTS

For many people, social media is a big part of their lives. Facebook, LinkedIn, Twitter, Instagram, Pinterest, and other social media sites act as a central hub connecting people with their friends, family, and memories.

Given their importance, rather than simply deleting your loved one's social media accounts, you might consider making them a legacy account.

Facebook, for instance, now empowers users to assign a legacy contact—someone who can look after your account after you die and who has the option to share a final message on your behalf or provide information about a memorial service, respond to new friend requests, update your profile pictures, and download a copy of what you've shared on Facebook. And, according to Facebook, they may add additional capabilities for legacy contacts in the future.

You may prefer to remove information from the web. Presently, Google, Facebook, Microsoft, AT&T, Sprint, Verizon, and T-Mobile have certain procedures in place for authorizing some form of access to the deceased's online accounts and email. There are procedures in place to allow a custodian to provide the user, or the user's personal representative, with access to the content.

While you can take down a deceased person's content, beware that in the absence of prior user consent, you will need a court order to view and have access to the emails or content.

A company at www.beyond.life has a helpful article, "What to Do with Social Media Accounts After a Loved One Dies." Check it out.

TRANSFER VEHICLE OWNERSHIP

If you're going to transfer the ownership of any vehicles owned by the decedent, you must first locate the title for each one. If the title is lost, apply for a duplicate title in the name of the deceased. The duplicate title may then be used to transfer vehicle ownership.

In many states, ownership of registered vehicles may automatically be transferred to the surviving spouse or children under age twenty-one. A surviving spouse or child transferring a registration to their own name may receive credit for the unexpired portion of the deceased's registration. Some state governments even allow the survivors to keep the same license plates; however, title and transaction fees still apply.

When there is no will, estate, surviving spouse, or surviving minor child, the next of kin may complete the transfer. A copy of the death certificate is required. For more information about the specific process for transferring ownership, contact your local Department of Motor Vehicles.

CHANGE OR CANCEL UTILITY ACCOUNTS

Utilities include gas, electricity, water/sewer, garbage collection, cable, internet access, etc. If the decedent's name is on the utility account, contact the company to change or cancel the account. They often don't need proof of death to make this change, but this varies by company.

REDIRECT PROPERTY TAXES

If the decedent and the survivor jointly owned property, the estate will likely transfer the property tax to the survivor.

Attend to Personal Affairs

MODIFY HOME AND AUTO INSURANCE

If necessary, contact the appropriate insurers to modify accounts with proper names. Check the mortgage or car title for the name of the insurance company. You may or may not need proof of death to modify the name of the insured.

CHANGE OR CANCEL OTHER ACCOUNTS

Where there are existing accounts with grocery stores, pharmacies, libraries, discount wholesale stores, department stores, pet stores, hardware stores, office supply stores, bookstores, and electronic toll collection services such as E-ZPass and SunPass, contact the appropriate company to cancel any accounts no longer used or update accounts with the name of the surviving spouse or child. You usually don't need proof of death to do this.

COMPLETE DECEDENT'S UNFINISHED BUSINESS

If the death was quick or unexpected, it's likely your loved one left unfinished business. It's important for you complete, return, cancel, or pick up any of the various plans or activities in process. On the next page, we've started a list and given you space to add other items.

DEATH'S RED TAPE

TO-DO LIST

- ❑ Donate or sell clothes, eyeglasses, medical equipment, and supplies.

- ❑ Contact the DMA to stop unwanted mail and email.

- ❑ Contact the credit reporting industry to stop receiving credit card offers.

- ❑ Register your home and cell phone numbers with the Do Not Call Registry.

- ❑ Decide how to handle social media accounts.

- ❑ Transfer vehicle ownership.

- ❑ Change or cancel utility accounts.

- ❑ Redirect property taxes (if needed).

- ❑ Modify home and auto insurance policies.

- ❑ Cancel open retail credit card accounts.

- ❑ Cancel or change names on existing loyalty program accounts such as with your grocery store, pharmacy, library, discount wholesale stores, department stores, pet store, hardware store, office supply store, bookstore, etc.

Attend to Personal Affairs

❑ Cancel or change names on electronic toll collection services.

❑ Pick up dry cleaning or tailoring, shoes, skis, etc.

❑ Return library books, videos, DVDs, etc. (Note: any fines are a debt of the estate.)

❑ Return recent purchases that are unused or no longer needed and cancel purchases on layaway.

❑ Cancel future appointments with doctors, dentists, or other services.

❑ Cancel vacations or other preplanned events.

9

AVOID IDENTITY THEFT

IDENTITY THEFT OCCURS WHEN SOMEONE OBTAINS AND USES YOUR personal information, such as your name or Social Security number, without your knowledge, to commit fraud or theft. The identity thief can use your information to fraudulently apply for credit, file taxes, steal the title to your home, or get medical services.

The 2021 Identity Fraud Study, released by Javelin Strategy & Research, found that identity fraud cost Americans a total of about $56 billion in 2020, with about 49 million consumers falling victim.

While companies usually have security standards and procedures in place to prevent unauthorized access to customer information, you should still take your own precautions. Here are some steps you can take to avoid becoming a victim of identity theft.

TWO SOURCES OF IDENTITY THEFT

You hear about it all the time, "XYZ Co. had a data breach." This traditional form of identity theft is where cybercriminals hack into a private database and steal personally identifiable information and use it for their own gains. This form of theft accounted for about $13 billion in losses in 2020 and accounted for about 23 percent of all identity theft.

Shockingly, most of the theft (about 77 percent) was begotten directly from the consumer! This is where criminals interact directly with consumers to steal their information through methods such as robocalls and phishing emails. Victims of these scams lost $1,100 on average, according to Javelin. Now let's talk about what you can do to minimize these risks.

PROTECT THE DECEASED'S INFORMATION

- In obituaries, don't include the deceased's birth date, place of birth, last job, or address.

- Immediately send death certificate copies by certified mail to the three main credit reporting agencies to request a "deceased alert" be placed on the credit report.

- Report the death to the Social Security Administration and the Department of Motor Vehicles.

- Starting the month after the death, check the deceased's credit report for suspicious activity at annualcreditreport.com.

PROTECT YOUR PERSONAL INFORMATION

- Only give out your Social Security number when necessary.

- Don't carry your Social Security number in your wallet or write it on notepads or checks.

- Don't respond to unsolicited requests by phone, mail, or online for your personal information, such as your name, birthday, Social Security number, or bank account number.

- When you enter your password or PIN number on computers and ATMs, shield the keypad so the information stays private.

- Shred papers such as receipts, credit offers, account statements, and expired credit cards to prevent Dumpster divers from obtaining your personal information.

- Drop paid bills directly into U.S. Postal mailboxes or at the post office, not in your home mailbox.

- Collect mail promptly and don't leave it sitting in your mailbox. If you're going to be away from home, have someone check and bring in your mail or ask the post office to put it on hold.

- Don't ever sign blank forms.

- Verify beneficiary information on life insurance and retirement accounts on a regular basis.

- Pay attention to your billing cycles and contact the company if your bills or financial statements are late.

- Destroy or black out the labels on prescription medicine before you discard the container.

- Don't share your health insurance information with anyone who offers free health services or products.

PROTECT YOUR ELECTRONIC INFORMATION

Protect Online User IDs and Passwords

Create strong passwords, especially for credit, bank, and email accounts. Don't use your Social Security number, date of birth, or mother's maiden name as a PIN or password. Instead, think of a special phrase and use the first letter of each word as your password, substituting some numbers for words or letters. For example, "I love to see my grandkids!" could become "Il2cmGK!"

Also, don't have your web browser store your passwords, as they aren't very secure. Anyone with access to your web browser can find them. Alternatively, you might want to consider a secure online password vault such as lastpass.com. These services are incredibly convenient, and most experts believe they are extremely secure.

Control Access to Your Computer

Set up a user password on your computer. Remember that your browser history files will automatically record recent web pages visited as well as specific access information. If someone were to have access to your personal computer, they may also have the same access to web accounts previously established by you or the decedent.

Establish More Than One Email Address

Use one email address for personal correspondence with friends and family and another for online transactions. Maybe even a third for finances. This way, you can delete any one specific email address in case you become suspicious or simply get bombarded with unsolicited email or spam.

Use a different password for each email address. Your email passwords should also be unique from your bank account and other financial passwords.

Don't Respond to Unsolicited Emails

Never respond to unsolicited emails from banks, credit card companies, online auctions, or convenient pay sites (like Venmo, PayPal, etc.) asking you to verify or update personal and account information. Scammers are constantly casting about for people's financial information by luring unsuspecting victims through a technique called phishing.

Phishing is a high-tech scam that uses spam email to trick consumers into disclosing their credit card numbers, bank account information, Social Security numbers, passwords, and other sensitive personal information. Consumers who provide their financial information in response to an unsolicited email could be at risk of identity theft.

If a company that claims to have an account with you sends you an email asking you to log on to their website, don't click on the link. Instead, go to the company's website directly and contact them through their customer service link or call the customer service number on your account statement.

It is also important to note intruders can disguise their email addresses, making it look different than it really is. To be sure you are replying to the right email address, hover your mouse cursor over it so you can see the actual email address. For instance, you might be looking for noreply@chase.com and be surprised to see that it is something like CHasEbnk_baNker@hotmail.com.

Don't Overshare

In the online environment, there are two common oversights. First, be sure to review your social media account's privacy settings at least once a year. Unless you specifically request otherwise, websites such as Facebook and Instagram often collect and share information about you. Secondly, avoid entering private information—credit card numbers, Social Security number, address, or date of birth—on a website that is not secure. To avoid this, look at the URL of the website. If it begins with "https" instead of "http," it means the site is secured (the "s" in https stands for secure). This assures you that your data is securely passed from your browser to the website's server.

Also beware of someone on the phone who is asking for personal information. If you need to, find out their name and where they are calling from and tell them you will call them back. Then look up their website, confirm their customer service number, and give them a call. Now you can be confident you are speaking with the right person.

Establish Notifications

Many financial institutions allow you to set up alerts so you can receive a notification via email or text when certain account activities occur. Common triggers for notifications include when a credit card payment is due, when a withdrawal exceeds a certain amount, or when an external transfer has been made. Choose the triggers that are meaningful to you.

Dispose of Electronics Safely

Before you get rid of your, or the decedent's, cell phone or computer, make sure you've removed all the personal information on it. For a computer, use a wipe utility program to erase and overwrite the entire hard drive. For a cell phone, do a factory reset. Then dispose of the electronics at an authorized dealer such as Best Buy.

Protect Against Hackers

Hackers are people who use their computers to gain unauthorized access to someone else's data. To help avoid your computer being "hacked," get a network security system (firewall) for your computer and keep your virus and spyware software up to date.

Use Wi-Fi Carefully

Public places such as coffee shops, hotels, shopping malls, airports, and many other locations often provide their customers free access to public Wi-Fi. Should you choose to connect your mobile device to their network, be aware that the information you send can be intercepted. Criminals can also hack into your mobile device, accessing your banking credentials, account passwords, and other valuable information. For this reason, you will want to take extra precautions:

- If your mobile device has a data plan and good reception, access the internet from that instead of using public Wi-Fi.

- Don't assume that every Wi-Fi link available to you is legitimate. It could be a bogus link that has been set up by a cybercriminal that's trying to capture valuable personal information from unsuspecting users.

- Avoid logging into websites that expose your identity, passwords, or personal information—such as social networking sites, online banking services, or any websites that store your credit card information.

- Make sure you protect all your devices with a reputable antimalware and security solution—and ensure that it's updated.

PROTECT YOUR MEDICAL INFORMATION

Medical identity theft happens when someone steals your health insurance information and uses your health insurance to get medical care, buy medication, or submit fake claims to Medicare in your name. This is why you have to show your ID or driver's license, along with your health insurance card, when you see a new doctor or healthcare specialist.

To prevent medical identity theft:

- Guard your Social Security, Medicare, and health insurance identification numbers. Only give them to your physician or other approved healthcare providers. In most cases, you don't need to give your Social Security number to healthcare providers; they use your health insurance subscriber number to bill your insurance.

- Regularly review your explanation of benefits form or Medicare Summary notes to make sure that the claims match the services you've received. Report any questionable charges to your health insurance provider or Medicare.

- Request and review your medical records for inaccuracies and conditions you don't have. This can be a good idea from a medical standpoint, too, as mistakes are sometimes made or important information, such as diagnoses or test results, aren't properly conveyed to the patient.

If you suspect you've been the victim of Medicare fraud, contact the U.S. Department of Health and Human Services Inspector General at 800-447-8477. If you have health insurance other than Medicare, contact your health insurance company.

MONITOR ACTIVITY ON CREDIT CARDS AND BANK ACCOUNTS

Monitor credit card bills and credit reports for unauthorized transactions. If you're a victim of identify fraud, you'll find purchases or withdrawals you never made on your credit card or debit account. Review your bank and credit card statements carefully as soon as you receive them. Report any unauthorized purchases to the credit card company immediately. Chances are you won't be required to pay for them.

Keep an Eye Out for Automated Double Billings

Many people now use their credit cards to pay for their satellite TV or cable, E-ZPass, Netflix, and other services that have a monthly service charge. As you check your credit card bills, be on the lookout for double billings or the same debit amount to the same service provider appearing twice in one month or one quarter.

REPORT FRAUD IMMEDIATELY

The first line of defense is to become more aware of identity theft and more aggressive in personally protecting yourself. A Federal

Trade Commission report said 26 percent of all identity theft victims discover the misuse within one week to one month after it begins, but 12 percent take over six months to discover the problem.

The faster you report any incidence of fraud, the faster the bank or credit card company can start to close accounts and clear your name right away. Furthermore, you should request that a fraud alert be placed on your credit report file so the credit bureau must contact you before any new credit can be approved.

To report identity theft, go to identitytheft.gov or call 877-438-4338 (TTY: 866-653-4261) and file a report with the Federal Trade Commission. Once you have an ID theft affidavit from the FTC, you can file a report with your local police department and get a police report. Together, these two documents are your identity theft report, which you can use as you resolve the issue with banks, creditors, and any other companies where fraudulent accounts were set up in your name.

Also contact each of the credit reporting agencies to place fraud alerts or freezes on your accounts so no one can apply for credit with your name and Social Security number:

- Equifax: 888-766-0008 or equifax.com

- Experian: 888-397-3742 or experian.com

- TransUnion: 800-680-7289 or transunion.com

CONSIDER PURCHASING FRAUD PROTECTION

In addition to the precautions mentioned above, you may wish to consider identity fraud protection via a property and casualty insurance carrier or implementing services such as those available through www.identityguard.com, www.identityforce.com, www.lifelock.com, and many others.

ORDER COPIES OF YOUR CREDIT REPORT EVERY YEAR

Because identity theft has become so rampant, federal law now allows you to obtain a free credit report online, by phone, or through the mail every year:

- Request your credit report online at www.annualcreditreport.com.

- Request your credit report by phone by calling 877-322-8228 (toll-free). You'll go through a simple verification process and then your reports will be mailed to you.

- Request your credit report by mail by filling out a request form and mailing it to:

  Annual Credit Report Request Service
  P.O. Box 105281
  Atlanta, GA 30348-5281

LIMIT HOW MANY CREDIT CARDS YOU HAVE

The more open credit cards you have, the higher your risk of identity theft. Sure, it's smart to always have a primary and a backup credit card, but don't hang onto more than one unused credit card. Having too many outstanding credit lines, even if not used, can hurt credit scores by making you look more potentially risky to lenders. Should you do this, consider closing the newer cards and keeping the older ones open. Closing older accounts can lower your average age of credit and hurt your score.

STAY INFORMED

For more information, contact the Federal Trade Commission's ID Theft Hotline at 877-IDTHEFT or 877-438-4338 toll-free or visit www.consumer.gov/idtheft.

The site contains helpful information for consumers and businesses on a variety of topics, including "phishing" scams, telecommunications fraud, internet fraud, and the theft of printed documents with personal information, as well as protecting employees from identity theft in the workplace.

The site also contains valuable consumer information on the steps to take if and when you find yourself a victim of identity theft.

DEATH'S RED TAPE

TO-DO LIST

❑ Remove your Social Security card from your wallet.

❑ Use a cross-cut shredder to dispose of credit card offers, credit card checks, and personal information.

❑ Create strong online passwords, with a combination of letters and numbers.

❑ Establish more than one email account.

❑ Establish notifications with your bank and financial accounts.

❑ Safely dispose of used cell phones and computers.

❑ Install a computer firewall and keep your virus and spyware software up to date.

❑ Regularly review your explanation of benefits or Medicare Summary.

❑ Request and review your medical records.

❑ Monitor activity on banks and credit cards and report fraud or identity theft immediately.

❑ Order yearly copies of your credit reports.

Avoid Identity Theft

❏ Keep an eye out for double automated billings on utilities, mortgage, and car loans.

❏ Consider purchasing fraud protection insurance.

❏ Cancel credit cards you don't use.

10

ESTATE PLANNING ESSENTIALS

As you've learned, there are many things in life that are not in our control. But one thing that is—or at least should be—is your estate plan.

A basic estate plan includes three things: a will, healthcare proxy, and power of attorney. Eventually, you might consider expanding upon your basic estate plan with things such as trusts, gifting of assets, and philanthropic strategies. For now, though, let's focus on the essentials.

LAST WILL AND TESTAMENT

Your last will and testament, or your will, is a legal document that formalizes your wishes regarding the distribution of your property and the care of any minor children.

It is important to understand that your will is specifically for the assets that do not allow for the naming of beneficiaries. Typically, this includes real estate, bank or investment accounts that don't have a designated beneficiary, collectibles, and personal belongings. It does not include life insurance, retirement accounts, or accounts with a transfer on death (TOD) contract. Those assets transfer directly without involving the will. Some people refer to this as "bypassing probate."

Before you meet with your attorney, take some time to think about:

- Who should care for your minor children, dependents, or pets?

- Who should inherit your assets, and in what proportions?

- Is there a charitable organization that you would like to leave money to?

- Who should be responsible for distributing your assets?

- How much is needed for your surviving spouse/partner to maintain his/her lifestyle?

Without a will, the state in which you reside decides how to distribute your assets to your beneficiaries according to its laws. This is known as dying intestate, and the resulting settlement process may not produce the results that you would prefer for your survivors. The last thing you want to do is leave your family with unnecessary stress after you die, so make sure to complete your will now.

HEALTHCARE PROXY

A healthcare proxy (sometimes referred to as a healthcare power of attorney) is of vital importance if a situation arises in which you are incapacitated and cannot make medical decisions for yourself. A properly executed healthcare proxy will empower someone you trust to make medical decisions on your behalf. This person is legally empowered to instruct doctors, nurses, and others involved with your care.

Sometimes, people get healthcare proxies confused with a living will, but they are not the same. A living will is only followed when you have a terminal condition and deals with life-prolonging procedures. It is certainly another valuable document.

POWER OF ATTORNEY

A power of attorney is a document that arranges for someone you trust to do business on your behalf or make legal decisions when you can't. In the absence of this document, your financial and legal matters can become gridlocked.

When you build your power of attorney (POA), be sure to include specific language that authorizes your agent to deal with your digital assets. This will provide your POA with the authority to manage your online accounts.

THE OVERLOOKED STEPS IN ESTATE PLANNING

In addition to completing your estate plan essentials, make sure to update your beneficiaries and account registrations.

Beneficiaries can be designated on your life insurance policies and retirement accounts—both individual retirement accounts (IRAs) and employer sponsored plans. This becomes especially important if the deceased was a designated beneficiary.

Although not as common, it's possible that your non-retirement accounts have a transfer on death (TOD) agreement. This document allows you to name account beneficiaries. At your death, assets with designated beneficiaries will transfer directly to your beneficiaries, bypassing the probate process. People often set up a TOD to save time and legal fees but, in some cases, it can contradict your existing estate plan. So, make sure you check with your attorney before executing any of these techniques.

Next, review your account registrations. Look at how they are titled and whose name is on the account.

If convenience and efficiency are important to you, consider changing the registration on one or more of your accounts to include a joint owner. While you are alive, the joint owner can assist you with paying bills and other banking chores. Additionally, if you are planning on transferring those monies to that person upon your death, it can make for a smoother transition.

This strategy isn't without risk, though. Keep in mind that one of the trade-offs is that this person now has access to your money. Also, if they get tangled up in a divorce or legal dispute, those monies become a part of it. Lastly, adding a joint owner may constitute a gift and contradict with your existing postmortem planning. So, to be sure you are making the right decision, check with your financial advisor and attorney.

KEEP YOUR ESTATE PLAN CURRENT

Consider your estate plan to be living documents. This means that you should continuously update them as needed. The catalyst for change is usually a life event such as marriage, divorce, death, or having children. However, it can also be a gradual change that has brought you to a new milestone such as a new level of net worth.

An incomplete or outdated estate plan can lead to unwelcome surprises for heirs. So, to be sure your estate plan is current, review it with your financial advisor or attorney at least every three years.

11

THE SOFT SIDE OF YOUR ESTATE PLAN

WHILE TRADITIONAL ESTATE PLANS SERVE A GREAT PURPOSE, THEY fail to address several practical, financial, and personal matters. For instance, they don't answer such questions as how to operate that old furnace, how the pets are cared for, what the purpose of the extra bank account was, or what should be done with the stamp collection. Oftentimes, survivors are also uncertain about last wishes such as whether the deceased wanted a burial vs. cremation, funeral arrangements, etc.

Proactively documenting this information requires some deep thought and a few hours of your time. On the other hand, imagine how difficult it would be for someone else to guess what your answers would be, especially if they had to do it during a crisis or upon your death.

There are a couple of ways in which this information can be shared. It can be as simple as writing your insights and wishes in a journal and then sharing it with the appropriate person. Should you prefer to be a bit more formal, you can complete what's known as a "Wisdom Will." It's a service I created and make available at www.mywisdomwill.com. Either way, using this tool or simply documenting your thoughts in a journal, sharing information about these matters is an invaluable gift.

WHAT TO DOCUMENT

Creating your Wisdom Will is more of a creative process than it is formal. Document anything you deem important and in any format you wish. Whatever the format, at least consider addressing the legal, practical, financial, and personal matters.

Legal Matters

The legal arrangements are all about determining who gets your stuff and how. It's a pretty basic concept but, with all of the moving parts, you'd be surprised how complicated it can get. To help your loved ones avoid confusion and frustration, share your insight on any or all of the four matters below.

How your overall estate plan is designed

Explain the desired outcome of your estate plan and how it's constructed to accomplish that. When your loved ones know your objectives and how your estate plan is designed, they can better execute the desired steps.

Explain:

- How the estate plan is structured. Do you have a will, trust, or other special arrangements?

- Who is responsible for what?

- What are your thoughts about charitable gifts and philanthropy?

Why it's designed that way

If your loved ones don't know why you made certain decisions, they have to guess at your intentions. This can cause pointless questioning and lead to family conflict.

Provide clarity around:

- Why did you structure your estate plan this way?

- Why did you choose certain people for their roles?

- Why are certain beneficiaries receiving an inheritance?

- Why are you giving money to charity, and why did you choose the charities you did?

Your business succession plan

If you own a business, share your high-level overview for how you wish things to play out in your business. This doesn't replace your business succession plan.

Address matters such as:

- Short- and long-term vision
- Equity ownership
- Leadership and management
- Management suggestions
- Company culture
- Employee and/or family dynamics

Practical Matters

Your loved ones will have enough to deal with after your death without worrying about where to find important paperwork or trying to figure out what you wanted.

Provide information for them on these practical topics.

Important people to contact after your death

Record contact information for the people you feel should be the first to know of your death and for important people who may be forgotten because of infrequent contact or long distance.

Your thoughts on your funeral/celebration of life

While the arrangements for your funeral, memorial service, or celebration of life are often made according to the needs and wishes of your survivors, it's worthwhile to express your opinions. Your loved ones will usually want to honor your wishes, but that can be hard in the turmoil of grief if they don't know what they are.

Topics you can address include:

- Do you want a funeral, a memorial service, or a celebration of life?

- Have you made any prearrangements? If so, where are they? Are they prepaid?

- Do you have a preferred location or funeral home?

- Do you want to be buried or cremated? Do you have a preferred cemetery or crematorium?

- Would you like an obituary printed and, if so, what should it include?

- Are there any psalms, readings, or songs you'd like at your service?

Organ donation and autopsy

In the minutes following your death, your loved ones need to be able to share your wishes about organ donation. Do you want some or all of your organs to be donated, and where do you have formal documentation of these wishes?

Additionally, if there is uncertainty about the cause of your death, the question may arise about whether or not to do an autopsy. What are your thoughts and feelings on that? Perhaps you feel an autopsy is warranted if it benefits medical research, solves a crime, or helps educate the medical field. Or perhaps you feel strongly that an autopsy should never be performed under any circumstances. Let your loved ones know.

Where you keep critical documents

Everyone has their own filing system that makes sense to them but may not work for anyone else. After your passing, there are many crucial documents that your loved ones will need. Let them know where they can find each of the following documents. Common locations include a safe or filing cabinet at home, a bank safety-deposit box, or with your attorney or financial advisor.

- Driver's license (or a photocopy)
- Passports

- Birth certificates/adoption papers
- Social Security card
- Service contracts
- Website access information
- Pet records
- Vaccination records
- Organ donor card
- Living will/healthcare proxy
- Durable power of attorney
- Stock/bond certificates
- Private loan papers
- Collectible coins, stamps, etc.
- Jewelry
- Trust agreement(s)
- Keys to safety-deposit box
- Copy of your employee contract

- Pension plan records

- Tax returns

- Receipts for home improvements

- Marriage license

- Divorce decree(s)

- Prenuptial/postnuptial documents

- Deed(s) for home(s)

- Title(s) for auto(s)

- Deeds for other property

- Credit cards

- Will

- Life insurance policies

- Disability insurance policies

- Long term care policies

- Death certificates

- Military papers

- Business agreements

Details about your online accounts

Our lives are increasingly lived online, especially our financial lives. Your loved ones will need to know how to access your online accounts, or they may experience frustration and financial mishaps.

Educate your loved ones about:

- **Online accounts**—which ones you have and for what purpose, including email, social networks, blogging sites, photo sharing sites, frequent flier accounts, shopping sites such as Amazon and eBay, credit card accounts, bank accounts, and online bill payment accounts such as the ones you have for your utilities.

- **Passwords**—where they are or the strategy you use to create and remember them, as well as the answers to your security questions.

- **Email**—your email accounts and how to handle them.

- **Social media**—your accounts and how to handle them. Should your loved ones keep them open in your legacy or close them?

- **Digital assets**—what digital assets you own, including video games, movies and music, and what you want your loved ones to do with them.

Household maintenance tips

If your surviving loved ones aren't familiar with how to maintain the household, leave them guidance. Consider topics such as:

- Technicians you trust for auto, plumbing, electrical, lawn, etc.

- Existing service contracts you have on appliances, furnace, etc.

- Seasonal chores that aren't obvious, e.g., cleaning a particular rain gutter

Insight about caring for children and adult dependents

This information is intended to be shared with caretakers, guardians, and trustees of your surviving minor children and adult dependents. Don't dictate how to raise the children or care for your elderly parents. However, you can share guidance to empower their caretakers or guardians to continue providing quality care.

Contact information for doctors and other medical providers, allergies and medical needs, and special care instructions can all be helpful. Behavioral observations are also important as they can help the caretaker handle things in a more meaningful and effective way.

Instructions on how to care for your pets

Your beloved pet(s) will have a new caretaker. This is your opportunity to share anything that might make the transition easier. Your Wisdom Will also goes a long way to ensure your pet(s) receive the care they deserve. Document information about your pet's:

- Daily care instructions
- Food, allergies, and medication
- Any medical conditions
- Behavioral conditions
- Veterinarian
- Caretakers that might be able to help care for your pet(s) or adopt them

Medical history that could impact your survivors

Family have many factors in common, including their genes, environment, and lifestyle. Together, these factors can give clues to medical conditions that may run in a family.

By noticing patterns of disorders among relatives, healthcare professionals can determine whether an individual, other family members, or future generations may be at increased risk of developing a particular condition.

For these reasons, share any notable medical history that might be beneficial for your loved ones and future generations to be aware of.

Financial Matters

Have peace of mind knowing you've safeguarded your loved ones from the financial despair that often plagues families after a death. Share your insight with your loved ones on these seven matters.

Overall state of finances and philosophies on money management

Give a high-level overview of your finances, with just enough information to bring your survivors up to speed with the general health of your finances and how you have chosen to manage them. You can also share your wisdom about how they can prudently manage money. Although your surviving loved ones may have their own approach, they might find your wisdom informative and helpful.

How your trusted financial advisor(s) can lend a hand

If you have a relationship with one or more financial advisors, share their contact information, the dynamics of your relationship, and an explanation of how they might be of assistance to your loved ones.

A list of savings, assets, and liabilities

Provide your loved ones detailed information about the amount and location of savings and investments as well as assets and liabilities. Also list any personal debt obligations to be paid or received.

If your assets and liabilities are documented somewhere already, let your survivors know where.

The practice of paying bills and managing debt

Do you have any personal financial debts that need to be repaid? Or other bills your survivors may not know about? Personal IOUs and other informal arrangements are common. Identifying them will help your survivors make sure that such obligations are satisfied.

Details about death benefits from your life insurance

What are all the potential sources of life insurance your survivors can collect? You may have traditional term or whole life insurance, but don't forget life insurance policies through your employer, union, credit card, mortgage provider, bank, university, etc.

List the insurance amounts, carriers, and agent information, or where your survivors can find this information.

The monetary death benefit provided by your life insurance can help in various ways. It might be a means of replacing lost income, paying estate taxes, covering the cost of college, paying off debts, etc. Provide some insight as to how you envisioned your life insurance benefit would help your loved ones.

Death benefits in addition to life insurance that your beneficiaries should collect

Beyond life insurance, your survivors might be eligible to collect other death benefits that provide a lump sum or income stream. This is not where you would list accumulated savings. Rather, this is for contractual benefits that are only paid upon your death.

They may come from:

- Social security and veteran benefits

- Pension plans

- Tax-deferred annuity

Income tax highlights that might save your survivors money

If you have an accountant, they are likely to know most of the information necessary to prudently manage your taxes. In such a case, you can list their name and a brief description of your relationship.

If you don't have an accountant or would like to share additional information, then list it. Examples include location of cost basis data, estimated tax projections, typical tax withholdings, RMD rules, tips on how to minimize taxes, whether or not the taxes are paid electronically (via online accounts), etc.

Personal Matters

You matter. Share with the world who you are and what you stand for. This information can have a profound impact on the lives of future generations and is too valuable to risk being lost. Below are seven things to consider writing about.

Your personal values and/or principles

This is your opportunity to shape the legacy for which you will be remembered. Share your perspective on what's important in life—your personal values and guiding principles. Unlike your physical property that can decay, disappear, or become extinct, your values can live forever. To cultivate some ideas, here are some questions to ponder:

- What is really important to you?

- What have you done in life to stand up for your values?

- How do you define true success?

- What does spirituality mean to you?

In your own life, you'll discover that the clearer your values become, the easier it is to make decisions about how to spend your time.

The lessons you have learned in your lifetime

Along the journey of life, you've learned invaluable lessons. If you have life lessons that have influenced the way you live your life, record them. It's a wonderful opportunity to positively impact future generations. To stimulate your thinking, ask yourself:

- Has there been an event (or person) that changed your life, and why?

- Are there any interesting or funny stories?

- Are there accomplishments or actions you're proud of?

- What are some things you have learned about love and relationships?

- What are some things you have learned about dealing with challenges and/or opportunities?

Special instructions regarding personal possessions of emotional value

Very often, personal possessions of emotional value are treasured by loved ones more than material goods and money. These are items such as photographs, family recipes, an old baseball glove, collectibles, a handmade cookie plate, etc. Because each item has a unique meaning, it might be best to let your loved ones choose who gets what. Nonetheless, if you would like to make suggestions or gift a certain item to a particular person, express your desires.

Cherished traditions that celebrate the uniqueness of your family or culture

Traditions are a valuable way to strengthen families, remind us of our heritage, and create lasting memories. New or old, share any traditions that you would like embraced by future generations.

Your family history is an important part of who you are

Knowing where you came from is a magical story that does more than satisfy curiosity. It helps you identify with who you are culturally and spiritually. Share a high-level overview of your family history and, if applicable, tell loved ones where they can go to obtain more information. If you have already obtained research through one of the many online ancestry services, be sure to leave login credentials.

Meaningful stories and memories

Record, share, and preserve the stories of your life to strengthen and build the connections with your loved ones and future generations. Whether it be from childhood or today or whether it's funny, sad, serious, or silly, your story matters. To take it a step further, consider visiting www.storycorps.org to learn about how you can vocally record your stories and have them preserved in the archive at the Library of Congress!

Leave your legacy letter

In the format of a personal letter, write whatever you'd like to share with your loved ones. Whether it be life lessons, principles, or emotions, share your blessings and speak from the heart.

To get inspired, read Barack Obama's legacy letter to his daughters and Richard Branson's "Letter to my Grandchildren." They are easily found by searching the internet.

SHARING YOUR WISDOM WILL

All this information is useless if nobody knows about it. This statement points out the obvious, but I've heard too many times, "I'll talk to them about it when the time is right." My advice is that the best time is now, before a crisis occurs. Organizing and sharing your final wishes now will safeguard your loved ones from the confusion, conflict, and despair that could otherwise follow your death.

12

PREARRANGE YOUR FUNERAL

MOST PEOPLE WOULD CONSIDER THIS TASK GOING ABOVE AND beyond, so don't feel obligated to prearrange your funeral. That said, it's surely a kind and considerate thing to do. There are some financial and logistical benefits too.

For instance, a short while ago, I attended a preplanned funeral. Not only had my friend purchased his casket and burial plot, but he also planned every detail of his funeral. He picked the person to deliver the eulogy and identified the songs, poems, and readings for the service. It was gratifying to know that he was remembered in a way that reflected his beliefs, his tastes, and his life.

You may wish to include your family in this process. After all, they'll be the ones directly affected and emotionally touched by the service. You should also let them know they're welcome to change the plans if it means they'll better represent everybody's wishes at the time of your death. Also keep in mind that it's prudent to review these plans every two to four years so they reflect your current desires at the time of your death.

Another reason to take control of your funeral arrangements is to ease the burden carried by your survivors and close friends. A typical funeral can cost between $8,000 and $14,000. If you don't make these major purchasing decisions in advance, your family will be asked to make them for you during a time of grief. You may have experienced this recently yourself. Your loved ones may feel guilty about cutting costs. And they may be overwhelmed by the number of decisions they'll need to make. Preplanning your funeral is one of the best ways to avoid possible confusion over the type of arrangements you'd want, and you may also save money.

The best way to prearrange a funeral is to sit down and talk with a trusted funeral director in your community. The Funeral Rule, enforced by the Federal Trade Commission, requires funeral directors to offer free consultations, itemized prices, and information about their goods and services. Once you've made your prearrangements, keep a copy of your plan and any pertinent paperwork in a safe place. Also, inform a close friend or relative about the arrangements you have made and where the information can be found.

Prearranging your funeral doesn't require you to prepay for it. While I am a huge proponent of prearranging your funeral, I often tell people that before prepaying for a funeral, ponder the advantages and disadvantages.

The Pros of Prepaying for Your Funeral

Ability to choose the funeral home with the right personality

Your loved ones will be working with the funeral home staff at a very emotional and stressful time, so it's important that you choose a funeral home that you believe they'll be comfortable with.

Ability to comparison shop for prices and services

The costs of caskets and professional services vary dramatically. Obtain a detailed price list from the funeral homes you're considering and take the time to compare your options to make an informed decision.

Protect against rising costs

Negotiate a contract that allows the purchase of tomorrow's merchandise and services at today's prices. This refers to an option you may have to prepay for your casket and funeral services. This cost protection guarantee, however, may not be as simple as it appears. Read the funeral service contract carefully, and if you're unsure about anything, ask questions. Also, each state has its own set of rules and regulations about how prepaid funeral expenses are handled. If you're unsure, call the state funeral directors association for more details. Choose a reputable funeral home and one with a long record of service to the community. If you don't know which funeral home to use, ask your friends and family for suggestions.

Reduce the size of the estate

Because this expense leaves less money in the bank, it means the size of the estate is a bit smaller. In some cases, this might result in less estate tax and/or may allow the individual to qualify for Medicaid benefits a touch sooner.

Shelter funds

If necessary, funds can be placed in an irrevocable trust for Medicaid or estate planning purposes.

Obtain peace of mind

Knowing that you'll be remembered exactly as you wish and ensuring that your loved ones won't be saddled with a heavy burden at a very vulnerable time will be a comfort to you today and as your time draws near.

The Cons of Prepaying for Your Funeral

Arrangements may not be portable

You may not be able to shift your arrangements to a new location if you leave your current city. Have the funeral home explain in their contract the boundaries of their service area and under what circumstances you can transfer the preneed contract to another funeral home if you were to relocate or if your death occurs outside of their service area.

Prices may not be guaranteed

If a funeral home didn't guarantee the prices of funeral costs and they inflate faster than the growth of the deposit, your loved ones will be forced to substitute less expensive merchandise or provide additional funding. Make sure the contract guarantees that if the merchandise or services selected aren't available at the time of need, merchandise or services of equal or greater value will be substituted at no extra cost.

If the prices aren't guaranteed, the contract should explain who will be responsible for paying any additional amounts that may be due at the time of the funeral. In the case of leftover funds, ensure that they'll be paid to your estate, or the funeral home will probably keep them.

Penalties may be lurking

If a prepaid funeral contract is cancelled, you may get back less than you paid. Not all states require funeral directors to provide a 100 percent refund. Furthermore, if payment is structured in installments, and payments are not completed before your death, the refund may be reduced by a sales charge that could be as high as 30 percent. Make sure cancellation penalties and refund policies are spelled out in the contract.

Costs can be misunderstood

In many states, part or all the interest earned on an account may be withdrawn each year by the seller as part of his administrative fees. Another typical misunderstanding is who will be responsible for paying taxes on the interest earned. Obtain a breakdown of all expenses in plain language and note in the contract who will be responsible for paying taxes on any income or interest generated by the invested funds.

The funeral home may not remain in business or it may get new owners

We are currently seeing a lot of changes in the funeral service industry. Small family-owned businesses are closing and/or selling to larger national firms. Wholesale funeral homes, promising to save you thousands of dollars, are moving into many cities. A very real concern for anyone prepaying their arrangements is that the seller of those funeral services may not be in business at the time of your death, or they may be under new ownership. Make sure that the prepaid funds are secured and that you or the account holder can withdraw them if the funeral home goes out of business or changes hands.

Your survivors may not know about the arrangements

The specifics of your prepaid funeral must be made known to family members; otherwise, that money can be lost. Make sure your funeral details are put in writing and a copy of the plan is kept in a safe place along with your other important papers. You should inform a family member, close friend, or even your attorney that prearrangements have been made, who they have been made with, and where the documents are kept.

Funding may be irrevocable

Before accepting an irrevocable agreement, carefully consider the implications of your decision. Irrevocable agreements are helpful when eligibility for Supplemental Security Income (SSI), Medicaid, or other public benefits are being determined, but they may limit flexibility. Many states now offer you the option of designating funeral accounts as irrevocable at a later date, should this protection be necessary.

If Social Security benefits aren't a primary concern, consider using a Totten Trust. This is an individual trust or savings plan earmarked for one's funeral. The consumer controls the account and can withdraw from it at any time. Usually, a sum of money equal to today's funeral costs is deposited in a passbook savings, certificate of deposit (CD), or money market account, payable to a beneficiary of the account holder's choice. These funds are available immediately at the time of death without the delay of probate. Accumulated interest helps cover costs increased by inflation.

Another alternative is life insurance with an increasing death benefit equal to the cost of the funeral. Funeral homes usually expect to be named the beneficiary, but that choice is up to you. Keep in mind, however, that the choice you make may determine whether or not the funeral home will freeze the costs at today's prices.

In summary, prepaying a funeral is a nice gesture, but caution should be taken. Maintaining control of the funds and/or making certain they are protected are considerations of paramount importance.

The National Funeral Directors Association (www.nfda.org) is an excellent source of information on this topic or, better yet, sit down with a trusted funeral director and talk about the pros and cons that apply to your unique situation.

APPOINT AN AGENT TO CONTROL DISPOSITION OF YOUR REMAINS

In some states, individuals are now able to legally assign an agent to control the disposition of their remains. Similar to a healthcare proxy or a living will, this legal document empowers the agent to make decisions on behalf of the individual—but specifically for taking care of the deceased's burial or cremation. In addition, the statute provides that an individual may give special directions, for example that they be cremated, that their body be buried in a particular grave at a specified cemetery, or that a particular funeral home handle the arrangements.

Appointing an agent to care for these matters is becoming popular for two reasons. First, even if a person's wishes are included in the will, an individual is usually buried or cremated long before a will is probated or even looked at. Second, with multiple marriages, same-sex relationships, and individuals who are domestic partners, the disposition of a loved one's remains is increasingly being litigated. Be sure to check with your local funeral director for more details.

Once again, planning your funeral or celebration of life isn't considered a must like creating an estate plan or Wisdom Will is. Nevertheless, those who do it often feel a sense of calm about their future death and ironically, a renewed enthusiasm to live a better life.

A perfect example of this rejuvenation is embodied in the phrase "live your dash," which comes from one of the most popular poems in the world, "The Dash" by Linda Ellis. It means to be mindful that life is short, and you should spend each day with passion and purpose. The poem ends with the line:

> **So when your eulogy is being read, with your life's actions to rehash, would you be proud of the things they say about how you lived your dash?**

DEATH'S RED TAPE

TO-DO LIST

- ❏ Draft or modify your will as needed.

- ❏ Draft a healthcare proxy and power of attorney.

- ❏ Update beneficiaries on your insurance contracts and retirement accounts.

- ❏ Consider putting individual accounts into jointly held accounts.

- ❏ Consider prearranging your funeral.

13

SAY YES TO LIFE

THIS IS WHERE THE FUN BEGINS. WITH THE DETAILS OF YOUR DEATH taken care of, you're better positioned than ever to focus on your future life.

For many, rewriting your future begins with the development of a new financial plan. The financial planning process begins with establishing goals and requires you to get clear about what you wish to spend your money on.

LEAN ON A TRUSTED FINANCIAL ADVISOR

Build your new financial plan with a trusted financial advisor or CERTIFIED FINANCIAL PLANNER™ professional. Knowledge and experience are important because the financial system is vast and complex. Rules and regulations around finance are ever-changing, and the internet publishes several misconceptions.

Doing it yourself can also be daunting as many aren't sure where to start or don't have the time required.

If you are searching for an advisor, examine their knowledge, experience, and reputation. Additionally, seek someone who collaborates and coordinates with other professionals. For instance, when a client of mine needs advice in an area that I am not an expert in, I'll introduce them to somebody who is. This is the case for professionals such as accountants, attorneys, bankers, healthcare consultants, senior care advisors, college planners, insurance experts, etc. Taking a team approach often results in a more sophisticated and meaningful plan.

Partnering with the right advisor is crucial. By doing so, you'll improve your opportunity to experience true financial freedom.

TAKE IT SLOW AND STEADY

Having been a survivor myself, I realize how important it is to manage the pace of financial planning. Before the death of your partner, it was likely that you made big money decisions together or bounced ideas off one another. Now, you're responsible for making decisions by yourself. For some, this could be empowering, and for others, it may be scary. Either way, recognize that you are in a new dynamic and so it is best to take your time. Otherwise, you may find yourself making hasty decisions you'll later regret.

Hasty decisions are prolific. A perfect example is when people change an account registration from joint to single. What on the surface appears to be a simple administrative fix might result in accidental tax ramifications. Another example is when people hurry up and pay off credit card balances, even if the credit card was in the deceased's name. This might feel like the right thing to do but can have unintended consequences. Doing this may be forgoing the opportunity to let the estate pay the debt or let creditors forgive it.

ADDRESS ESSENTIALS FIRST

There's no doubt that the loss of a partner can be an emotionally overwhelming and challenging time in one's life. This often makes decisions difficult. So, start the financial plan by only addressing the essentials. Keep your focus on regaining financial stability. The essential financial items include things like:

- Collecting survivor benefits

- Getting your finances organized

- Reviewing your financial obligations and income sources

- Establishing a budget

- Rewriting your will, healthcare directive, and power of attorney

During these first planning steps, I recommend you bring a friend or family member to meetings so they can take notes while you remain focused on the conversation with the planner. Whomever you bring will also be better suited to assist you with the tasks assigned by the planner.

Pointing out the obvious, you'll see that the essentials don't involve making major decisions. People often postpone major decisions for a year because they are not in the right frame of mind. To make a smart financial decision, you also need a good understanding of your finances.

FOCUS ON YOUR FUTURE

After you care for the essentials, you can look to planning for your future. For some, it can be hard to think of what your new life will look like, but give it a try. Some might even say that a financial plan without a vision is a futile attempt at organizing your finances. But with an understanding of what matters most to you and clear goals, it becomes meaningful. Hopefully, it will inspire you to spend your time and money on what you love.

EMBRACE FINANCIAL FREEDOM... AND LIFE

Until your financial plan is complete, you may feel a bit apprehensive about spending money. Many are concerned about whether their money will last. A successful financial plan, delivered by the right financial planner, has the power to transform your feelings of financial doubt to financial freedom. This doesn't mean that a good plan will let you spend as much as you want on whatever you want. Rather, it makes you aware of your financial capacity. This reduces anxiety otherwise associated with spending your money.

This is a game changer because it reassures you that it is okay to begin spending your time and money on what you love.

Seeing countless clients transform from financial doubt to financial freedom has been exhilarating. My hope is that you have the same experience so you, too, can say yes to life, create new memories, and live a life of abundance and joy.

AFTERWORD

When Joanne died, I put my life on hold. For months, life was consumed with sorrow and the burden of administrative details related to her death. As time went on and these challenges subsided, I was able to begin moving forward. I went back to work, attended social engagements, and introduced new activities into my life. When a daily routine set in, the structure was a welcome relief.

I learned not only how to continue with my life but created a new one. I married a wonderful woman, Kathy, who made me excited about living again. She and I were also blessed with two awesome children, our son Christopher and daughter Emily. And for you animal lovers out there, you can appreciate how important it is to mention my two black Labradors, Cooper and Louie, and my cat, Rex.

So, my final message to you is one of inspiration. Remember that while life may bring us unfair challenges, it can also bring unexpected blessings of which we never dreamed.

ACKNOWLEDGMENTS

I WOULD LIKE TO THANK THE THREE PEOPLE WHO INSPIRED ME TO write this book—my late wife, Joanne; my deceased mother, Bobbi; and my wife, Kathy.

The courage and kindness Joanne displayed throughout her life was a true motivation for me to embrace life and share quality time with people I love.

My mother—beyond being an awesome mom—was also a great role model. She always showed a genuine interest in helping others and never asked for recognition. She instinctively knew that the simple pleasure from lending a hand was much more rewarding than any pat on the back.

I would like to also thank my wife, Kathy. She rejuvenated me and got me excited about life again. We especially connected with our love for the outdoors and animals. And our children, Chris and Emily, are yet another blessing we share together. Kathy has also been very supportive of my passion to help people who have lost a loved one and supported my efforts to write this book.

Additionally, I appreciate the input from my financial planning clients who opened their hearts to share their endearing stories of survival. Their heartfelt experiences provided invaluable information and insight to ensure this book strikes a balance between being practical yet personal.

ADDITIONAL RESOURCES

THE FOLLOWING RESOURCES PROVIDE MORE INFORMATION ON various topics discussed throughout this book. To be sure of current numbers and addresses, please check the internet.

American Bar Association
www.americanbar.org

Career Gear (donations of men's clothing)
www.careergear.org

Department of Veterans Affairs
800-827-1000 or www.va.gov

Do Not Call Registry
www.donotcall.gov

Dress for Success (donations of women's clothing)
www.dressforsuccess.org

Federal Trade Commission's ID Theft Hotline
877-438-4338 or www.consumer.gov/idtheft

Fraud Insurance
www.identityfraud.com or www.javelinstrategy.com

Funeral Consumers Alliance
www.funerals.org or 800-765-0107

Funeral Consumers Alliance is a nonprofit organization dedicated to protecting a consumer's right to choose a meaningful, dignified, and affordable funeral.

Gift of Life Donation Initiative
www.organdonor.gov

The Grief Recovery Institute
818-907-9600 or www.grief.net

The Grief Recovery Institute offers an action program for moving beyond loss and a great series of articles that can help you get a clearer picture of what is true and accurate in relationship to both grief and recovery.

Internal Revenue Service
800-829-1040 or www.IRS.gov

Mark Colgan, CFP® professional
585-419-2270 or www.montagewm.com
or www.mywisdomwill.com

Additional Resources

Founding Partner, Montage Wealth Management, and Creator, www.mywisdomwill.com

National Funeral Directors Association
414-541-2500 or www.nfda.org

Social Security Administration
800-772-1213 or 800-325-0778 (TTY) or www.ssa.gov

GLOSSARY

Administrator
A person appointed by the court to supervise the handling of an individual's estate in the event that no will has been executed.

Affidavit
Any written document in which the signer swears under oath before a notary public or someone authorized to take oaths (like a county clerk) that the statements in the document are true.

Beneficiary
The named party who receives proceeds under an insurance policy, trust, or will.

Bond
A debt security, similar to an IOU. When you purchase a bond, you're lending money to a government, municipality, corporation, federal agency, or other entity known as the issuer.

Cash Value
The "savings element" in a permanent life insurance policy, which is the property of the policy owner.

Certificate of Deposit
A deposit with a specified maturity date and interest rate.

CERTIFIED FINANCIAL PLANNER™ Professional
Anyone can call themselves a financial planner, but only those individuals who have voluntarily taken the extra step to demonstrate their professionalism and high ethical standards can be certified by the Certified Financial Planner Board of Standards. Their accreditation indicates they are capable in financial planning as well as managing a client's banking, estate, insurance, investment, and tax affairs. Only those individuals can call themselves a CERTIFIED FINANCIAL PLANNER™ professional and use the CFP® designation after their name.

Codicil
A document that amends a will. It must be executed like a will and witnessed by two people not named as beneficiaries for any of the assets.

Creditor
Lender of monies.

Death Benefit
The proceeds of the policy that will be paid upon the insured's death.

Decedent
A person who has died. Also referred to as the deceased.

Dependent parent
A parent who is determined to be dependent under IRS standards and for whom an exemption can be claimed. See IRS Publication 501 for more information.

Disclaimer
The refusal, rejection, or renunciation of a claim, power, or property.

Estate Tax
A tax paid on property or assets owned at the time of death.

Executor/Executrix
An individual appointed through a will to administer and distribute property upon the testator's death. "Executor" is the male version and "executrix" is the female form of the word.

Fiduciary
An individual who manages property or acts on behalf of another individual and is placed in a position of trust.

Guardian
An individual who has the legal right and duty to take care of another person or another's property because that person cannot legally handle these responsibilities.

Healthcare Proxy (Healthcare Power of Attorney)
A legal document that allows you to appoint someone to make medical decisions if you become unable to competently make them for yourself.

Interment
The act of burial.

Individual Retirement Account (IRA)
A retirement account that may have been established by an employed or self-employed individual.

IRA Rollover
A provision enabling a retiree or anyone receiving a lump-sum payment from a pension, profit-sharing, or salary-reduction plan to transfer the amount into an IRA.

IRA Beneficiary Distribution Account (IRA BDA)
A retirement account established by a beneficiary. An inheritance where the deceased's name remains on the account.

Intestate or Intestacy
The state of dying without a legal will where a probate court oversees asset distribution.

Irrevocable
Unable to be amended, altered, or revoked.

Legacy
A combination of life facts, photos, video clips, favorite stories, powerful memories, and wisdom that one can package together as a gift to future generations of one's family.

Medicaid
A joint federal and state program that helps with medical costs for people with low incomes and limited resources.

Medicare
The federal health insurance program for people sixty-five years and older. Certain people who are younger but who have disabilities and/or serious illness may also be eligible.

Living Trust
A legal arrangement, established during an individual's lifetime and which is fully amendable and revocable by its creator, under which a trustee holds title to property with the obligation to keep or use it for the benefit of the beneficiary. Living trusts are commonly used as vehicles to avoid probate.

Living Will
A legal document allowing you to express your wishes as to healthcare treatment, not estate planning. It makes clear what measures you want taken—or not taken—to keep you alive if you're seriously ill.

Mutual Fund
A financial intermediary that allows a group of investors to pool their money together under a fund manager who buys and sells securities with a predetermined investment objective.

Power of Attorney
A document that authorizes someone to act on another's behalf.

Power of Appointment
Typically used with trusts, it gives an individual the power to decide which beneficiaries receive distributions and in what amounts.

Principal
The total amount of money being borrowed or lent.

Probate
The process of proving that a will is genuine and distributing the property accordingly.

Roth IRA
A type of individual retirement account that allows contributors to make annual contributions and to withdraw the principal and earnings tax-free under certain conditions.

Stock Certificate
A document reflecting legal ownership of a specific number of stock shares in a corporation.

Testamentary Trust
A trust that is created upon the death of the decedent pursuant to the terms of the will through or as a result of the probate process.

Trust
A legal arrangement in which an individual holds title to property, subject to an obligation to keep or use it for the benefit of the beneficiary.

Trustee
A person who holds money or property for the benefit of another.

Supplemental Security Income (SSI)
Monthly benefits paid by the Social Security Administration to individuals who qualify because of limited income and resources or who are disabled, blind, or age sixty-five or older.

Surrogate's Court
County or state court that handles cases involving the affairs of decedents, including administration of wills, estates, and trusts.

Transfer Agent
Individual or institution that a company appoints to handle the ownership transfer of securities.

Transfer on Death (TOD)
The process of changing the title of a security from one name to another upon the death of one of the titleholders.

Urn
Container designed to hold an individual's cremated remains.

Will
A legal document through which a person declares or designates how their possessions will pass after death.

INDEX

accountants, meeting with, 13–14
administrators, definition of, 177
adult dependents, 30, 144–145
advisors, notification of, 3
affidavits, 15, 122, 177
Affordable Care Act Health Insurance, 44
airline bereavement fares, 6
American Council of Life Insurers, 37
American Legion, 47
annualcreditreport.com, 123
art works, valuation of, 84–85
ashes, locations for, 8–9
assets
    changing names on, 83
    digital, 64–65
    disclaiming, 83
    distribution of, 87
    donation of, 85
    estate plans and, 130, 147
    inventory of, 78
    liquid, 82
    liquidation of, 85
    living trusts, 88–89, 181
    not subject to probate, 80–81
    review of, 59–66
    sentimental, 64–65
    title transfers, 89
    unfreezing, 79
    valuation of, 84–85
Association of National Advertisers (ANA), 101
attorneys, 11–13, 17, 59–66, 129–131
auctions, 85
automobiles, 4, 53, 63, 107
autopsies, estate plans and, 140

bank accounts, 77, 80–81, 83, 121, 147
bank correspondence, 52
beneficiaries
    definition of, 177
    designation of, 15
    eligible, 94
    of IRAs, 132
    notification of, 81
    reports to, 88
    verification of, 114
benefits, for survivors, 27–48
bills
    double billing, 121
    estate plans and, 147
    organization of, 53
    paperwork organization and, 59–66
    paying of, 67–74, 85–86, 114
birth certificates, 53, 77
boats, transfer of ownership, 63
bonds, 61, 77, 177
brokerage accounts, 61, 80–81
budget worksheets, 18–21
burglaries, protection against, 6
burials, 7–9, 46–47
business associate notification, 3
business succession plans, 138

Career Gear, 98
cars. see automobiles
cash flow, financial reserves and, 17–21
cash value, definition of, 177
cell phone contracts, 69–70
cemeteries, 7–8, 46–47
certificate of deposits, 178
Certified Financial Planners™, 95, 178, iv, ix, xiii
charitable pledges, 71
charities, donation to, 98
Chase Military Services, 62
check registers, 77
children, estate planning and, 29–30, 144–145
Children's Health Insurance Plan, 44

INDEX

Civilian Health and Medical Program, VA (CHAMPVA), 46–47
Civil Service Retirement System (CSRS), 6, 36
COBRA options, 43–44
codicils, 50, 178
collectables, valuation of, 84–85
Computer Fraud and Abuse Act, 56
computers, 115. see also online accounts
contracts, 52, 68–70, 130, 141, 144, 155, 157–158
correspondence, 49–54, 51, 52. see also documents; paperwork
credit cards, 37, 68, 121, 124
creditors, 68, 81, 85–86, 178
credit reporting agencies, 10–11, 102, 112, 123
cremation, choice of, 8–9
cybercriminals, 111–127

death benefits, 178
death certificates, 9, 53
debts, 83–86, 147
Deceased Do Not Contact List (DDNC), 101
deeds, 52
Department of Motor Vehicles, 113
dependents, care of, 144–145, 179
Determining the Value of Donated Property (IRS 561), 99
digital assets, 64–65, 144
Direct Marketing Association, 101, 103
disclaimers, 88, 179
divorce certificates, 78
documents. see also paperwork
  collecting, 76–78
  filing systems for, 140–143
  shredding of, 113
Donate Life America, 4
donations, 4–5, 97–100
Do Not Call Registry, 103
Dress for Success, 98
driver's licenses, 4
Drug Enforcement Agency National Prescription Take-Back Day, 100
dying intestate, 130

Electronic Death Registration, 10
electronic information, protection of, 114–119
electronics, disposal of, 118
eligible designated beneficiaries (EDB), 94
email accounts, 55–56, 104, 115–116, 143
emails, unsolicited, 116–117
Employer Identification Numbers (EINs), 82
employers, 3, 37, 42, 51

enhanced death benefits, 63
Equifax Information Services LLC, 11, 102, 122
estate accounts, 82
estate documents, 50
estate plans
  asset reduction and, 156
  design of, 136–137
  documentation of, 136–152
  essentials, 129–133
  financial matters and, 146–152
  funeral arrangements, 139–140
  household maintenance and, 144
  overlooked steps in, 132–133
  reviews of, 133
  sharing information about, 135–136
estates
  claims against, 81
  insolvent, 85–86
  size of, 84–85
  transfer of, 15–16
estate taxes, 17–21, 73, 86–87, 179
executors/executrixes
  definition of, 179
  notification of, 3, 14
  role of, 75–76
  selection of, 130
Experian, 11, 102, 122

families, Social Security benefits for, 27–35
family histories, 151
family members, help from, 5
Federal Employee's Retirement System (FERS), 6, 36
Federal Estate Tax Form 706, 86
Federal Trade Commission, 124–125, 154
fiduciary, definition of, 179
filing systems, 50
financial accounts, 60, 117–118, 146
financial advisors, 36, 147, 163–164
financial decisions, postponement of, 17
financial planning, 13, 164–166
flexible spending accounts (FSAs), 45
flowers sent, keeping track of, 4–5
Ford Credit, 69
fraud, 121–123
friends, help from, 5
funeral directors, 3, 8–10, 154
Funeral Rule, 154
funerals
  agents assigned to, 160–161
  arrangements for, 139–140
  costs of, 5, 154
  paying the expenses of, 68

Index

prearrangements for, 5, 153–162
prepaid, 5, 155–160
preparation for, 5–9

Garn-St. Germain Depository Institutions Act of 1982, 70
gifts, keeping track of, 4–5
glossary, 177–183
grief, 1–2, 17–21, 22–23
guardians, definition of, 179
guest books, 5

hackers, protection against, 118
Health and Human Services Inspector General, U.S. Department of, 119–120
healthcare power of attorney, 131, 179
healthcare proxies, 131, 179
health insurance options, 43–46
Health Savings Accounts (HSAs), 45–46
heirs, notification of, 81
home improvement records, 52
home insurance, modification of, 107
hospitals, notification of, 3

identity theft, 111–127
identitytheft.gov, 122
income taxes, 71–73, 149
Individual Retirement Accounts (IRAs), 60
  beneficiaries of, 132
  definition of, 180
  disclaiming, 95
  distribution options, 93–96
  rollovers, 180
  tax treatment of, 41
Information for Survivors, Executors, and Administrators, 72–73
inheritance taxes, 86
insurance agents, notification of, 36
insurance membership corporation, 38
insurance policies, 52, 77, 82–83
interment, definition of, 180
Internal Revenue Services (IRS), 7, 41–42, 87, 98–99
internet domain names, 65
intestate, 180
investment information, 54, 59
irrevocable, definition of, 180

joint-ownership, 15, 62

legacies, definition of, 180
legacy letters, 152
Letters of Administration, 79

life insurance
  beneficiary verification, 114
  claims process, 36–41
  estate plans and, 148
  mortgages and, 68
  paperwork, 51
  proceeds from, 86
  sample letter to, 39–40
  tax treatment of proceeds, 41
  ways to receive benefits, 38–39
living trusts, 88–89, 181
living wills, definition of, 181
loans, life insurance and, 68

mail, collection of, 114
mail solicitations, 101
marriage certificates, 78
Martindale-Hubble directory, 13
Medicaid health insurance, 44, 180
medical equipment, 99–100
medical histories, 145–146
medical information, protection of, 119–120
medical supplies, 99–100
Medicare, 181
Medicare fraud, 119–120
memorial services, 5–9
memories, estate plans and, 152
military papers, 53, 78
Military Survivor Programs, 62
Missing Money, 21
mortgage lenders, insurance from, 37
mortgages, 61–62, 70. see also real estate
mutual funds, 181
"My Insurance Log," 37
mywisdomwill.com, 5

NAIC Life Insurance Policy Locator services, 38
National Association of Unclaimed Property Administrators, 21
National Cemetery Administration, 6
National Funeral Directors Association, 160
notes payable, transfer of, 70
notes receivable, current, 61–62

obituaries, information in, 112
online accounts, 55–56, 70–71, 114–115, 117, 143
organ donation, 3–4, 140
organization of paperwork, 49–57, 76–78
outstanding receivables, collecting, 83–84

INDEX

paperwork. see also documents
  location of, 138
  organization of, 49–57, 51–54
passwords, 113, 114–115, 143
payable on death (POD) accounts, 80–81
paycheck stubs, 51
Peace of Mind program, 69
pension plans, 41, 148
personal affairs, 97–109
personal information, protection of, 113–114
personal loans, 62
personal possessions, 97–99, 151
personal property titles, 77
pets, estate plans and, 145
phishing, 116
PIN numbers, protection of, 113
Powers of Appointment, 50, 181
powers of attorney (POAs), 50, 77, 131–132, 181
prescription medicine, 99–100, 114
principals, definition of, 182
probate, 15, 182
probate courts, 75–76, 79
property deeds, 52
property taxes, redirection of, 106
property transfers, 15–16

real estate
  deeds, 77
  insurance for, 82–83
  liens against, 70
  paperwork, 54
  titles for, 62, 77
resources, 173–175
retirement accounts, 60, 114. see also Individual Retirement Accounts (IRAs)
retirement benefits, 42
Roth IRAs, 182

safe-deposit boxes, 7, 16, 140–143
salaries, unpaid, 42
scammers, 116–117
Setting Every Community Up for Retirement Enhancement (SECURE) Act, 93
sheltering funds, 156
sick pay, 42
small estates affidavits, 15
social media accounts, 104–105, 143
social organizations, insurance from, 37
Social Security Administration (SSA), 9–10, 27–35, 113, 148
Social Security cards, 53, 77
Social Security numbers, protection of, 113

Social Security survivors, 28–30
solicitations, 101–103, 115–117
spam, 103, 115–116
stock certificates, 77, 182
stock transfers, 61
subscriptions, 70
Supplemental Security Income (SSIs), 182
Surrogate's Court, 76, 79, 184
survivor benefits, 27–48
sympathy cards, 4–5

tax deduction, 7
tax-deferred annuities, 148
tax information paperwork, 51
testamentary trusts, 182
transfer agents, 183
transfer on death (TOD) accounts, 80–81, 183
TransUnion, 11, 102, 122
trust agreements, 50, 77, 156
trustees, definition of, 182
trusts, definition of, 50, 77, 88–89, 156, 181, 182

unclaimed funds, checking for, 21
unfinished business, 107
unmarried children, 29–30
urns, definition of, 183
U.S. Income Tax Return for Estates and Trusts, 87
utility accounts, 106

vacation pay, 42
vehicles, 63, 68–69, 105–106, 113
Veterans Affairs, Department of (VA), 46–47
veterans' benefits, 6, 46–47, 148
Veterans of Foreign Wars, 47
visitors, keeping track of, 4–5

websites, income-earning, 65
Wi-Fi security, 118–119
wills, 50, 77
  definition of, 183
  dying intestate, 78, 130
  estate planning and, 129–131
  executors/executrixes, 75–76
  filing of, 15–16
  location of, 5
  submission to probate, 79
  witnesses to, 14
workers' compensation benefits, 42
World Medical Relief, 99–100
www.healthcare.gov, 44
www.organdonor.gov, 3

ABOUT THE AUTHOR

HAVING EXPERIENCED THE UNEXPECTED DEATH OF HIS BELOVED WIFE, Joanne, Mark learned at the early age of thirty-one the fragility of life and the importance of proper planning. A sad yet valuable life experience, it helped cultivate his success as a comprehensive and compassionate wealth manager.

EXTENSIVE CREDENTIALS

Mark Colgan has been in the financial services industry for two decades. Prior to his career, Mark earned his BS in finance from the Rochester Institute of Technology.

- CFP® professional

- FINRA Series 7 registration
  (General Securities Representative)*

- FINRA Series 63 registration
  (Uniform Securities Agent State Law)*

- FINRA Series 65 registration
  (Uniform Investment Adviser Law)*

- Life and health insurance licenses

- Registered representative and investment advisor representative of Commonwealth Financial Network®, the largest privately held independent broker/dealer in the nation, to take advantage of all the services and resources they offer

A CITED EXPERT

- Nationally recognized specialist on the topic of legacy planning

- Articles published in *U.S. News and World Report*, the *Journal of Financial Planning, American Association of Individual Investors,* and *Money Adviser,* a consumer reports publication

About the Author

- Previously cited by FOX News, CBS MarketWatch, Oprah and Friends, Morningstar.com, and other mainstream media